# ESSENTIAL IDIOMS IN ENGLISH

# ESSENTIAL IDIOMS IN ENGLISH

## A NEW REVISED EDITION

*With Exercises for*
*Practice and Tests by*
Robert J. Dixson

PRENTICE HALL REGENTS, Englewood Cliffs, NJ 07632

*Cover design:* Paul Gamarello.
*Interior design:* Suzanne Bennett & Associates.

*Cartoon credits:*
Page 1 by Arnie Levin; page 5 by Catharine O'Neill;
page 6 by Donald A. Orehek; page 10 by Michael
Tillyer; page 13 by Leonard Herman; page 17 by Arnie
Levin; page 21 by Aaron Bacall; page 23 by Michael
Dater; page 27 by Michael Tillyer; page 30 by Michael
Dater; page 31 by David R. Howell; page 35 by Steve
Kell; page 45 by Michael Tillyer; page 52 by Donald A.
Orehek; page 56 by Jack Cassady; page 64 by Arnie
Levin; page 71 by Jerry Van Amerongen; page 75 by
Frank Cotham; page 79 by Michael Tillyer; page 86 by
Catharine O'Neill; page 91 by Donald A. Orehek; page
95 by Andy Wyatt; page 99 by Jerry Van Amerongen;
page 112 by Donald A. Orehek; page 115 by Sylvio
Redinger; page 123 by Michael Tillyer; page 135 by
Frank Cotham; page 142 by Catharine O'Neill; page 147
by Jerry Van Amerongen.

ISBN  0-13-286329-4  01

Published by
Prentice-Hall, Inc.
A Division of Simon & Schuster
Englewood Cliffs, New Jersey 07632

Printed in the United States of America

10  9  8  7  6  5  4

# CONTENTS

to go off the deep end . . . to lose (one's) touch . . . to have going for . . . on the double . . . on hand

# FOREWORD

Idiomatic expressions are accepted as part of normal, everyday speech. Teachers of English as a foreign or second language have long recognized the importance of idioms as a means of adding grace and precision to speech and writing. Understanding idioms also greatly enhances listening comprehension. *Essential Idioms in English* is the first comprehensive text to attempt to teach idioms by means of extensive practice exercises.

Using idiomatic expressions fluently is never an easy task for the ESL or EFL student. Attempts to translate literally from the native tongue invariably lead to confusion and the student is often forced to resort to circumlocution.

The student may learn grammar and, with time, acquire an adequate vocabulary, but without a working knowledge of such idioms as *inside out, to get along, to call for, to look up, to look over,* etc., even the best student's speech will remain awkward and stilted.

To be sure, complete control of the idioms of any language requires years of study and practice. But this should not discourage the student. The alert teacher will make this study an integral part of the regular teaching of grammar and vocabulary.

Of course, the idioms for study should have practical value and be well within the student's grasp. Such expressions as *to carry coals to Newcastle* or *to wash one's dirty laundry in public,* while very colorful, do not help the student achieve the goal of gaining fluency.

For this reason, only basic idioms have been included in this book, hence the name *Essential Idioms in English.* Furthermore, it was decided not to burden the student with theorizing about the nature or origins of idioms. There is little attempt to define idioms here except to assume that an idiom is a phrase which has a meaning different from the meanings of its component parts. This explains why an idiom cannot be translated literally from one language to another without some change in its meaning or connotation.

For the purposes of this book, *two-word verbs* are included in the general category of idioms. A two-word verb is a verb whose meaning is altered by the addition of a particle. *To look,* for example, may become *to look up* or *to look over.* When a two-word verb can be separated by a noun or a pronoun, the symbol (S) is inserted in the definition. Examples of both separated and non-separated usages are included in the sentences illustrating separable two-word verbs.

Experienced ESL and EFL teachers will likely endorse the selection of idioms in this text, especially in the first (elementary) and second (intermediate) sections. In the third (advanced) section, however, it should be appreciated that any selection of this level must be arbitrary because the range is so great. While some teachers might include some idioms, other teachers would have others which they would favor. *Essential Idioms in English* is an attempt to be as representative as possible.

Mention should be made of a unique feature that adds to the usefulness of this book: Appendix II is a listing of all the idioms in the book with their equivalents in Spanish, French, and German. Having these equivalents should give the student a surer grasp of the meaning of the English idioms and greater confidence in using them.

The second revision of *Essential Idioms in English* contains several new additions to replace those idioms which, as all vocabulary does, have become outdated. It also includes a number of cartoons that help demonstrate the idioms graphically in order to maximize student understanding and to enliven a study that is at times tedious and difficult.

# LESSON 1

1. **to get on:** (to enter, board. Note also how *get* or *catch* is used.)
   1. I always *get on* the bus at 34th Street. I *catch* it at 8:30 a.m.
   2. William *gets on* the subway at the same station every morning. He *gets* the one on 8th Avenue marked "AA."

2. **to get off:** (to leave, descend from)
   1. Helen *got off* the bus at 42nd Street.
   2. At what station did you *get off* the subway?
   3. Do you usually *get off* there?

3. **to put on:** (to place on oneself—usually said of clothes) (S)*
   1. Mary *put on* her scarf and left the room.
   2. Why is John *putting on* his coat and hat?
   3. *Put* your hat *on* before you leave the house.

4. **to take off:** (to remove: said particularly of clothes) (S)
   1. John *took off* his hat as he entered the room.
   2. Is Helen *taking off* her coat because it is too hot in the room?
   3. *Take* your sweater *off* in this warm room.

5. **to call or call up:** (to telephone) (S)
   1. I forgot to *call up* Mr. Jones yesterday, although I promised to *call* him exactly at 3 o'clock.

---

*The symbol (S) indicates that an idiom is *separable*—that a direct object may be placed between the verb and the prepositional particle. In these cases, examples are given with the idiom both separated and unseparated. See Appendix I, page 167 for further details.

*I'm sorry, I never see anyone personally. However, you may call me from that phone.*

Drawing by Levin; © 1981 The New Yorker Magazine, Inc.

    **2.** *Call* me *up* tomorrow, Jane: we'll arrange to have lunch together.

**6.** to turn on: (to start, begin) (S)
    **1.** Please *turn on* the light; this room is dark.
    **2.** Someone *turned on* the radio while we were out.
    **3.** Do you know who *turned* it *on*?

**7.** to turn off: (to stop, terminate, extinguish) (S)
    **1.** Shall I *turn off* the stereo or are you still listening to it?
    **2.** Please *turn off* the light when you leave the room.
    **3.** Shall I *turn* the oven *off*?

**8.** right away: (immediately, very soon)
    **1.** Dad says that dinner will be ready *right away,* so we'd better wash our hands.
    **2.** Can William come to my office *right away*? I must see him immediately.
    **3.** It will only take me a minute to repair your shoes; they'll be ready *right away.*

**9.** to pick up: (to take, especially using one's fingers) (S)
    **1.** Harry *picked up* the newspaper which was on his desk.
    **2.** Why didn't you *pick up* that pencil which was on the floor?
    **3.** I would have *picked* it *up* if I had noticed it.

**10.** at once: (immediately, very soon, right away)
    **1.** He was in a hurry, so he asked me to come to his office *at once.*
    **2.** I want you to send this telegram *at once;* it's urgent.

**11.** to get up: (to arise, to move from a lying or sitting position to a standing one) (S)
    **1.** I *get up* at 7 o'clock every morning.
    **2.** What time does your brother usually *get up*?
    **3.** The man was so weak that the nurse was unable to *get* him *up* from the chair.

**12.** at first: (originally, in the first instance)
    **1.** *At first* he seemed to find English difficult, but later he made good progress.
    **2.** *At first* I thought it was Sheila at the door, but then I saw that it was Betty.

**A.** Substitute an idiomatic expression for the word or words in italics.* Make any necessary changes in the form of the word in parentheses. Some substitutions may require other grammatical changes as well.

1. He *arises* at the same time every morning.

   (get _____)
   Example: He *gets up* at the same time every morning.

2. She *telephoned* me very late last night.

   (call _____)

3. Helen said that she was going to mail the letter *immediately.*

   (right _____)

4. Be sure to *extinguish* the light before you leave the room.

   (turn _____)

5. Pat *placed on* herself her new hat while looking in the mirror.

   (put _____)

6. *Remove* your overcoat and sit down for a few minutes.

   (take _____)

7. *Originally* I thought it was Bob who was calling me.

   (at _____)

8. We *boarded* the bus at Broadway and 79th Street.

   (get _____)

9. The bus was so crowded that we had difficulty in *leaving.*

   (get _____)

10. John *took with his fingers* the pencil which was lying on the floor.

    (pick _____)

**B.** Answer these questions, making use of the idiomatic expressions studied in this lesson.

1. Where do you *get on* the bus or subway every morning?

2. Where do you usually *get off?*

3. Is it easy or difficult to *get on* a crowded bus?

---

*In Number One above, the verb *arises* is in italic type.

4. Is it easy or difficult to *get off* an uncrowded bus?
5. Which of your friends *called you up* last night?
6. Who did you *call up* last night?
7. Did Henry say that he would return *right away* or later this evening?
8. Do you generally *put on* your hat and coat when you leave your apartment?
9. When do you generally *take off* your hat and coat?
10. When you arrive at school each day, do you immediately *put on* your hat and coat or *take off* your hat and coat?
11. What do you do when you leave school each day?
12. If you want to hear some music, do you *turn on* or *turn off* the radio?
13. What do you do when you finish using the radio or television?
14. When do you usually *get up* every morning?
15. When do your brothers and sisters *get up*?

# LESSON 2

1. **to wait for:** (to expect, await)
   1. We will *wait for* you on the corner of Main and 10th Street.
   2. We *waited for* him more than an hour, then we finally left when he didn't come.
2. **at last:** (finally, after a long time)
   1. We waited for hours and then the train arrived *at last*.
   2. Now that I am 16, *at last* I can drive my parents' car.
3. **as usual:** (as always, customarily)
   1. George is late for class again *as usual*. This seems to happen every day.
   2. *As usual*, Dora won first prize in the swimming contest this year. It was her third victory in a row.

*As usual, no one's interested in your economic theories.*

4. to find out: (to get information, discover, learn) (S)
   1. I was unable *to find out* the name of the man who called.
   2. Will you please try *to find out* what time that train arrives?
   3. I'll try *to find* it *out*.

5. to look at: (to direct the eyes toward, watch)
   1. The teacher told us *to look at* the blackboard and not at our books.
   2. I like to walk along a country road and *look at* the stars at night.

6. to look for: (to search for, seek, try to find)
   1. He has spent an hour *looking for* the pen which he lost.
   2. I have lost my gloves. Will you help me *look for* them?
   3. We have *looked* all over *for* you.

7. all right: (satisfactory, correct. Sometimes used to mean "Yes.")
   1. He said that it would be *all right* to wait in his office until he returned.
   2. Would it be *all right* with you if I pay back that money tomorrow instead of today?
   3. Let's watch TV tonight. *All right,* let's do it.

8. right here, right now, right there, etc.: (exactly here, immediately, there, etc.)
   1. He said that he would meet us *right here* on this street corner.

2. *Right then* when he lowered his eyes I saw very clearly that he was not telling the truth.
3. Let's do it *right now;* I'm tired of waiting.

9. little by little: (gradually, by degrees, slowly)
    1. If you study regularly each day, *little by little* your vocabulary will increase.
    2. His health seems to be improving *little by little.*

10. tired out: (extremely weary) (S)
    1. I have worked very hard today and am *tired out.*
    2. He was *tired out* after his long trip to California.
    3. The long walk *tired* her *out.*

11. to call on: (to visit)
    1. Last night several friends *called on* us at our home.
    2. How many salesmen *call on* Mr. Evans every day?

12. never mind: (don't worry about it, do not bother or pay attention to it)
    1. When he spilled his drink on my coat, I said, "*Never mind.* It needed to be cleaned anyway."
    2. When William wanted to return the money he owes you, why did you say: "*Never mind!* Wait until next week when you receive your paycheck"?

*Is it all right with you if we finish this first!*

**A.** Substitute, in place of the italicized word or words, the corresponding idiomatic expression partially indicated in parentheses.

# EXERCISES

1. Nan is *seeking* the wallet she lost yesterday.

   (look _____)

2. *As always,* Doug is late again for the lesson.

   (as _____)

3. Did you *discover* what his name was?

   (find _____)

4. I am *extremely tired* after all that physical exercise today.

   (tired _____)

5. He said that he would wait for us *exactly here* on this corner.

   (_____ here)

6. Some old friends of my father's *visited* us last night.

   (call _____)

7. *Gradually* his English seems to be getting better.

   (little _____)

8. They are *awaiting* their brother who is arriving tonight on the five o'clock train.

   (wait _____)

9. We waited for 45 minutes and *finally* the waiter brought our food.

   (at _____)

10. He said that it would be *satisfactory* for us to call again later.

    (all _____)

**B.** Answer these questions, making use of the idiomatic expressions studied in this lesson.

1. Why were you *tired out* after your long walk in the park yesterday?

2. Which friends *called on* you last night?

3. What friends do you yourself expect *to call on* next week?

4. When Helen offered to help you with your homework, why did you say, *"Never mind"*?

5. Is your vocabulary increasing rapidly or only *little by little*?

6. What is the teacher *looking for* in her desk?

7. If you lose something, do you *look for* it or *look at* it?

8. What time was it when you last *looked at* your watch?

9. Do you dislike having to *wait for* someone who is late?

10. How long did you have to *wait for* the bus this morning?

11. Did Mary say that we should *wait for* her *right here* in the lobby?

12. How can you *find out* what movies they are showing in your neighborhood?

13. How do you *find out* what time the picture begins?

14. Did you do your homework last night *as usual*?

15. Did the teacher say that it was *all right* for us to write our exercises in pencil, or did she say that we should use a pen?

16. What are all those people in the street *looking at*—an accident or a parade?

# LESSON 3

1. **to pick out**: (to choose, select) (S)
   1. I want *to pick out* a good book to give my brother as a Christmas present.
   2. Which magazine did you *pick out* to give Anne?
   3. If you want me to treat you to a dessert, *pick* one *out*.

2. **to take one's time**: (to work or go leisurely, avoid hurrying)
   1. There is no hurry. You can *take your time* doing those exercises.
   2. William never works rapidly. He always *takes his time* in everything that he does.

3. **to talk over**: (to discuss, consider) (S)

1. We *talked over* Carl's plan to put in air conditioning, but could not come to a decision.
2. They should *talk over* their vacation plans before they leave.
3. Before I accepted the new job offer, I *talked* it *over* with my wife.

4. to lie down: (to recline, take a lying position)
   1. If you are tired, why don't you *lie down* for an hour or so?
   2. The doctor says that Grace must *lie down* and rest an hour every afternoon.

5. to stand up: (to rise, to take an upright or standing position after being seated.)
   1. When the president entered, everyone in the room *stood up*.
   2. Please *stand up* when we call your name.

6. to sit down: (to take a seat or a resting position after standing)
   1. After standing for so long, it was a pleasure to *sit down* and rest.
   2. We *sat down* on the park bench and watched the children play.

7. all day: (the entire day, continuously through the day)
   1. I have been working on my income-tax form *all day*. I started after breakfast, and now it's time for bed.
   2. It's been raining *all day*. We haven't seen the sun since yesterday.

8. by oneself: (alone)
   1. Francis translated that French novel *by himself*. No one helped him.
   2. Paula likes to walk through the woods *by herself*. Her brother prefers to walk with a companion.

9. on purpose: (for a reason, intentionally)
   1. It was no accident. She arrived late *on purpose*.
   2. Do you think he spilled the soup *on purpose* so that he wouldn't have to eat it?

10. to get along: (to do, succeed, make progress)
    1. Juan is *getting along* very well with his English. He learns more every day.
    2. How is Mr. Holmes *getting along* in his new job? Does he like it?

*My Lord, it doesn't make any difference which stairs you use.*

11. **to make no (any) difference**: (to be of little or equal importance)
    1. When I asked him whether he wanted to go in the morning or in the afternoon, he said, "It *makes no difference* to me."
    2. Does it *make any difference* to you whether we have our lesson at 2 o'clock or at 3 o'clock? No, I don't care.

12. **to take out**: (to remove, extract) (S)
    1. Did the dentist *take out* your tooth or did he fill it?
    2. Every night Jim *takes* his dog *out* for a walk.

# EXERCISES

A. Substitute in place of the italicized word or words the corresponding idiomatic expression partially indicated in parentheses.

  1. I don't like to go to the movies *alone*.

    (by _____)

  2. Suddenly the thief *removed* a gun from his pocket and began to shoot.

    (took _____)

3.  We *discussed* his plan for hours.

    (talk _____)

4.  I always like *to recline* for a half-hour after lunch.

    (lie _____)

5.  It is always difficult for me *to select* a good present for my mother.

    (pick _____)

6.  Jack always *works leisurely* in everything that he does.

    (take _____)

7.  How is Marie *doing* in her new French class?

    (get _____)

8.  It *is of little importance* to him whether he passes his English examination or not.

    (make _____)

9.  I am sure that he didn't leave that cigarette there *intentionally*.

    (on _____)

10. We spent *the entire day* looking for a new apartment.

    (all _____)

**B.** Answer these questions, making use of the idiomatic expressions studied in this lesson.

1.  How are you *getting along* in English?
2.  Which student in your class seems to be *getting along* best?
3.  How is your friend *getting along* in his new job?
4.  Do you prefer to go to the movies *by yourself* or with someone?
5.  Does your friend live *by himself* or with someone?
6.  Did you come to the United States *by yourself* or with your family?
7.  Do you like *to talk over* your personal problems with someone or do you prefer to decide these things *by yourself*?

8. Is it easy or difficult for you *to pick out* presents for your friends?

9. Does someone help you *to pick out* your clothes or do you like *to pick* them *out by yourself?*

10. What did you do *all day* yesterday?

11. When the "Star-Spangled Banner" is played, what should one do: *stand up* or *sit down?*

12. Do you *take your time* when you are writing an examination or do you prefer to finish quickly?

13. What did the teacher just *take out* of the drawer of the desk?

14. During the lesson do you prefer to sit in front of the room or in the back—or doesn't it *make any difference?*

15. Why must Ellen *lie down* for several hours each afternoon?

# LESSON 4

1. to take part in: (participate, join)
   1. Martin was sick and could not *take part in* the meeting last night.
   2. I did not want *to take part in* their argument, so I remained silent.

2. at all: (to any degree, in the least—generally used only in a negative sense with "not" or "hardly")
   1. He said that he did not have any money *at all*.
   2. When I asked her whether she was tired, she said, "Not *at all*. I'm full of energy!"

3. to look up: (to search for a word, a price, a telephone number, etc., especially in a dictionary or catalog where one must turn pages) (S)
   1. Students should *look up* new words in their dictionaries.
   2. Ellen said that she didn't know Robert's number but

*Well, so far so good.*

that she would *look* it *up* in the telephone directory.
3.  *Look* this date *up* in the encyclopedia, please.

4.  **to wait on:** (to serve, attend to—in a store or restaurant)
    1.  A very pleasant young clerk *waited on* me in that shop yesterday.
    2.  The waitress asked, "Have you been *waited on* yet?"

5.  **at least:** (a minimum of, no fewer or less than)
    1.  Students should spend *at least* two hours on their studies every night.
    2.  Gloria has been sick in bed for *at least* two months.

6.  **so far:** (until or up to the present time)
    1.  *So far,* this year has been the best for my family's business. I hope our good luck continues.
    2.  How many idioms have we studied in this book *so far,* 42 or 142?

7.  **to take a walk:** (to go for a walk, promenade)
    1.  Last evening we *took a walk* around the park.
    2.  It is a fine day. How would you like to *take a walk* along Arlington Boulevard?

8.  **to take a seat:** (to sit down)

1. Ms. Johnson asked me to come in and *take a seat* across from her.
2. "Please *take your seats*," the usher said. "You are blocking the aisle."

9. **to try on:** (to test or put clothing on before buying) (S)
   1. He *tried on* several suits and finally picked out a blue one.
   2. Why is it necessary *to try on* shoes before buying them?
   3. *Try* this brown skirt *on* next.

10. **to think over:** (to consider carefully before deciding) (S)
    1. I'll *think over* your offer and give you my answer tomorrow.
    2. You don't have to decide this matter at once. You can *think* it *over* and give me your decision next week.

11. **to take place:** (to happen, occur)
    1. The meeting *took place* in Constitution Hall.
    2. Where did the accident *take place*?

12. **to put away:** (to set aside out of sight, return something to its proper place) (S)
    1. After John finished reading the report, he *put* it *away* in the desk.
    2. Mother always told us *to put* our toys *away* when we finished playing.
    3. *Put* your book *away*; it is time for lunch.

# EXERCISES

A. Substitute, in place of the italicized word or words, the corresponding idiomatic expression partially indicated in parentheses.

1. You'll have to *search for* his number in the telephone book.

   (look _____)

2. He asked me to come in and *sit down*.

   (take _____)

3. The accident *occurred* on the corner of Park Avenue and 32nd Street.

   (take _____)

4. I will *consider* your plan and give you an answer next week.

    (think _____)

5. The pitcher did not feel well enough to *participate* in the game.

    (take _____)

6. *Up to the present* we have enjoyed our trip very much.

    (so _____)

7. He doesn't speak English *to any degree*.

    (at _____)

8. The mother said to the child, "You have played long enough with your toys. Now please *return them to their proper place*."

    (put _____)

9. Did a man or a woman *attend to* you in that store?

    (wait _____)

10. The salesman said to me. "Please *test* this coat for size."

    (try _____)

11. You ought to spend two hours *as a minimum* in the fresh air every day.

    (at _____)

12. In the evening we *promenaded* down Fifth Avenue.

    (take _____)

B. Answer these questions, making use of the idiomatic expressions studied in this lesson.

    1. How many new words do you have *to look up* in your dictionary every day?

    2. If you do not know someone's telephone number, where do you *look it up*?

    3. In what century did the American Revolution *take place*?

    4. Where did the accident *take place*?

    5. How many invitations have you sent out for your party *so far*?

    6. *So far*, who is the best student in your English class?

7. What is the difference between *to wait for* a person and *to wait on* a person?

8. Why was Herbert not able to *take part in* the meeting last night?

9. Approximately how many different countries *take part in* the United Nations General Assembly each year?

10. Does your friend speak English well, with some difficulty, or not *at all?*

11. When you go to a store to buy something, do you prefer to have a man or a woman *wait on* you?

12. How many pairs of shoes did you *try on* before buying the pair that you are now wearing?

13. Are you a neat person? Do you always *put* your things *away* after using them?

14. Do you like or dislike *taking part in* discussions about politics?

# LESSON 5

1. to look out: (to be careful or cautious)
   1. *"Look out!"* Jeffrey cried as his friend almost stepped in front of the moving car.
   2. Why did the driver tell Ida *to look out* as she was getting off the bus?
   3. *Look out* for cars turning in your direction.

2. to shake hands: (to exchange greetings with a clasp of the hands)
   1. I introduced them and they *shook hands*.
   2. When two people meet for the first time, they usually *shake hands*.

3. to think of: (to have an opinion about) (S)
   1. What did you *think of* the movie you saw last night?
   2. I don't *think* much *of* him as a baseball player.

4. to get back: (to return) (S)
   1. Mr. Harris *got back* from Chicago last night.
   2. When do you expect *to get back* from your trip?
   3. Can you *get us back* by five o'clock?

*Why couldn't you teach me to
shake hands like all the other dogs?*

5. to catch cold: (to become sick with a common cold–weather
   sickness of the nose and/or throat)
   1. If you go out in this rain, you will surely *catch cold.*
   2. How did she ever *catch cold* in such warm weather?

6. to make up (one's) mind: (to decide)
   1. Sally has not *made up her mind* about which college to
      go to.
   2. When are you going to *make up your mind* where you
      are going to spend your vacation?

7. to change (one's) mind: (to alter one's decision or opinion)
   1. We have *changed our minds* and are going to Canada
      instead of California on our vacation.
   2. Matthew has *changed his mind* about buying a new car
      at least three times.

8. for the time being: (for the present, temporarily)
   1. *For the time being* my sister is working in a department
      store. She hopes to work as an actress soon.
   2. We are living in a hotel *for the time being*, but later we
      will try to find a small apartment.

9. to get over: (to recover from or to accept a loss or sorrow)
   1. It took me more than a month *to get over* my cold, but
      I'm well now.
   2. I do not think he will ever *get over* the death of his wife.

10. **to call off: (to cancel) (S)**
    1. The game was *called off* on account of darkness.
    2. When the snow began we had to *call off* our ice-skating party.
    3. At first the workers planned to strike, but later they *called it off.*

11. **for good: (permanently, forever)**
    1. Ruth has gone back to California *for good.* She will not return to the East.
    2. Is your friend finished with school *for good?* Won't he ever resume his studies?

12. **in a hurry: (hurried, in a rush)**
    1. Alex is *in a hurry* to catch his train; he's late.
    2. She is the kind of person who moves so quickly that she always seems to be *in a hurry.*

# EXERCISES

A. Find and underline the expression given in parentheses that corresponds to the italicized idiom. For example, in Sentence 1 underline *canceled* since it is the corresponding term to *called off.*

1. If a meeting is *called off,* it is
   (begun, crowded, interesting, canceled).

2. If someone is *in a hurry,* he is
   (tired, rushed, ill, happy).

3. To *get over* something is to
   (like it, buy it, come over to it, recover from it).

4. When I say that someone finally *got back,* I mean that he finally
   (left, returned, woke up, rested).

5. *To make up one's mind* is
   (to wait, to decide, to get up, to leave).

6. If someone is in the United States *for good,* he is here
   (to do good, temporarily, to rest well, permanently).

7. If someone says *"Look out!",* you should
   (put your head out the window, be careful, sit down, go ahead).

8. If I say that I *don't think much of this book,* it means that I
   (never read it, seldom think about it, don't like it).

9. *For the time being* means
   (always, in the near future, for the present).

10. People *shake hands* when they
    (argue, are introduced to each other, become angry).

**B.** Answer these questions, making use of the idiomatic expressions studied in this lesson.

1. Do you often or seldom *catch cold?*

2. Do people *catch cold* more often in the winter than in the summer?

3. How long does it usually take you *to get over* a cold?

4. When children are introduced to each other, should they *shake hands* the way adults do?

5. Has your friend gone back to his country *for good* or only temporarily?

6. Has George stopped smoking *for good* or has he only quit for a month or so?

7. Why did your aunt tell her child *to look out* before he crossed the street?

8. Why was the baseball game *called off* this afternoon?

9. Why did Mrs. Smith *call off* her trip to Detroit?

10. When will Charles *get back* from Chicago?

11. When did Melba *get back* from Florida?

12. What do you *think of* your teacher?

13. What do you *think of* the weather we are having this week?

14. Is it easy or difficult for you *to make up your mind* about most things?

15. If you have once *made up your mind*, do you often *change your mind* later?

16. Can you now give good examples of these idioms in sentences: *get on, get off, get up, get back, get along?*

# LESSON 6

1. **according to**: (in a manner that matches or agrees with, on the authority of)
   1. The students were ranked *according to* height, shortest to tallest.
   2. *According to* my dictionary, you are using that word incorrectly.

2. **to hang up**: (a. to place upon a hook or coat hanger; b. to replace the telephone in its cradle) (S)
   a. He *hung up* his coat in the closet.
   b. The operator told me *to hang up* and dial the same number again.

3. **to count on**: (to depend on, rely on)
   1. We are *counting on* you to help us with today's assignment.
   2. Don't *count on* Frank to lend you any money because he has none.

4. **to make friends**: (to win or gain friends)
   1. Patricia is a very shy girl and does not *make friends* easily.
   2. During the cruise Ronald *made friends* with everyone on the ship.

5. **out of order**: (not in working condition)
   1. The elevator was *out of order* and we had to walk to the tenth floor.
   2. We could not use the telephone because it was *out of order.*

6. **to get to**: (to arrive at a place, home, work, etc.)
   1. I missed the bus and didn't *get to* the office until ten o'clock.
   2. This train *gets to* Chicago at eleven o'clock tonight.
   3. What time did you *get* home from the movie last night? (Do not use the preposition *to* with *home* or *there*.)

7. **at times**: (sometimes, occasionally)
   1. *At times* they play like champions, but usually they are a losing team.
   2. *At times*, she feels a little better, but then she becomes very weak again.

8. **to look over**: (to examine) (S)
   1. I want *to look over* these exercises before I give them to the teacher.

*At times, I feel people don't listen to me.*

   **2.** You should never sign anything without *looking* it *over* first.

**9.** to have (time) off, to take (time) off: (to have free time, not to have to work)
   **1.** We *have time off* for a coffee break every morning.
   **2.** He works only five days a week and *has every Saturday and Sunday off.*
   **3.** I expect to *take the whole summer off.*

**10.** to keep on: (to continue)
   **1.** Al *kept on* talking although the teacher asked him several times to stop.
   **2.** They *kept on* playing their radio until three o'clock in the morning.

**11.** to put out: (to extinguish) (S)
   **1.** You can *put* your cigarette *out* in that ash tray.
   **2.** The firefighters worked hard but were not able to *put out* the fire.
   **3.** Be sure to *put out* the light before you leave. All right, I'll *put* it *out.*

**12.** all of a sudden: (abruptly, without warning)
   **1.** *All of a sudden* Ed appeared at the door. We weren't expecting anyone.
   **2.** *All of a sudden* Millie got up and left the house with no explanation.

# EXERCISES

**A.** Find and underline the expression given in parentheses that corresponds to the italicized idiom.

1. *To have time off* is to
   (be busy, have free time, be ill, be without a job).

2. *To keep on* doing something is to
   (stop doing it, continue doing it, begin doing it).

3. *At times* means
   (often, never, on time, occasionally).

4. When I say that I *got* there at ten o'clock, I mean that at ten o'clock I
   (left there, waited there, arrived there, stayed there).

5. *To count on* someone is to
   (like him, arrest him, doubt him, depend upon him).

6. If something is *out of order,* it is
   (messy, not in working condition, modern, old-fashioned).

7. *According to* means
   (with a rope, by a musical instrument, on the authority of).

8. *To look over* something is to
   (wait for it, look it up, examine it, purchase it).

9. When I *put out* my cigarette, I
   (light it, smoke it, enjoy it, extinguish it).

10. *All of a sudden* has the same meaning as
    (later, early, unexpectedly, slowly).

**B.** Answer these questions, making use of the idiomatic expressions studied in this lesson.

1. *According to* your dictionary, what does "joyous" mean?

2. Why does Carlos *keep on* studying English if he finds it so difficult?

3. How long did it take the firefighters *to put out* the fire?

4. Where may I *put out* my cigarette?

5. Why do you say that you can never *count on* William to help you with anything?

6. If we tell Ella our secret, can we *count on* her not to tell anyone else?

7. How many days each week do you *have off* from work?

8. Do you always *have Saturdays off?*

9. Do you always *look over* your homework before you give it to the teacher? Do you ever ask a friend to *look it over* for you?

10. Is the elevator in your building often *out of order*?

11. What do you do when you find the telephone *out of order*?

12. What time did you *get to* school this morning?

13. What time did you *get* home last night?

14. Can you give good examples of these idioms in sentences: *look over, look up, look out, look at, look for*?

# LESSON 7

1. to point out: (to indicate) (S)
   1. What important buildings did the guide *point out* to you in your trip around the city?
   2. The teacher *pointed out* the mistakes in my composition.
   3. A friend *pointed* the president *out* to me.

*Dear, there's something I think I'd better point out.*

2. to be over: (to be finished, ended)
   1. After the dance *was over,* we all went to a restaurant.
   2. The chairman said that the meeting *would be over* in an hour. Actually, it ended in 45 minutes.

3. to be up: (to be ended—said only of time)
   1. "The time *is up,*" the teacher said at the end of the test.
   2. We will have to stop practicing on this piano now; our time *is up* and the next student wants to use it.

4. on time: (exactly at an appointed time, not late)
   1. I thought Margaret would be late for our 12:00 appointment, but she arrived right *on time,* walking in at exactly noon.
   2. Did you get to work *on time* this morning or were you late?
   3. The 5:15 train to Jamaica left *on time.*

5. in time: (within or sometime before an appointed time or a deadline, soon enough)
   1. We got to the movies just *in time* to see the beginning.
   2. Did you get to the station *in time* to catch your bus?

6. to get better, worse, etc.: (to become better, worse, etc.)
   1. Heather has been sick for a month, but now she is *getting better.*
   2. Even though we've been giving our dog this medicine, he seems to be *getting worse.* I'm afraid he's going to die.

7. to get sick, well, tired, busy, wet, etc.: (to become sick, well, tired, busy, wet, etc. Different adjectives may be used after *get* in this construction)
   1. Gerald *got sick* last January and has been in bed since then.
   2. Every afternoon at about 4 o'clock I *get* very *hungry,* so I eat some fruit.

8. had better: (it is advisable to, it would be better to. Most often used in contracted form such as *I'd better, you'd better, she'd better, he'd better, we'd better, they'd better*—Always followed by the base form of the main verb in a sentence.)
   1. I think *you'd better* speak to Mr. White immediately about this matter; it's very important.
   2. The doctor told the patient that *he'd better* go home and rest for a few days.

9. would rather: (to prefer to always followed by the base form of the main verb in a sentence.)

1. *I'd rather* go for a walk than watch TV tonight.
2. *Would* you *rather* have your next lesson on Monday or on Tuesday?

10. by the way: (incidentally, something else that one thinks of.)
    1. *By the way*, have you seen the new picture that's playing at Radio City this week?
    2. He told me, *by the way*, that he never planned to remarry.

11. to figure out: (to calculate, to study carefully in order to understand) (S)
    1. This letter is so badly written that I can't *figure out* what the writer is trying to say.
    2. How long did it take you *to figure out* the cost of that new product?
    3. Her job is interesting and it pays well, and yet Moira is quitting. I can't *figure* her *out*.

12. to put off: (to postpone) (S)
    1. We didn't have our meeting today; it was *put off* until next week.
    2. There is an old saying which goes, "Never *put off* until tomorrow what you can do today."
    3. If Tom can't come to the conference, let's *put* it *off* until tomorrow.

# EXERCISES

A. Find and underline the expression given in parentheses that corresponds to the italicized idiom.

1. If I say that the meeting *is over*, I mean that the meeting has
   (just begun, ended, been interesting, been called off).

2. If I say that *I'd rather* wait, I mean that I
   (like to wait, refuse to wait, prefer to wait).

3. If I say that, after studying the message, I finally *figured it out*, this means that at last I
   (answered the message, understood it, put it away, picked it up).

4. If the month *is up*, that means that the period of one month has
   (ended, begun, seemed long, been very warm).

5. *To put off* something means to
   (look for it, put it in place, have it, postpone it).

6. *To get sick* means to
   (recover, become ill, be well)

7. If the doctor says that *you'd better* do a certain thing, this means that
   (you must do it, you are going to do it, it is advisable that you do it).

8. *To point out* something is to
   (need it, see it, look it up, indicate it).

9. *By the way* is a synonym for
   (however, at last, incidentally, immediately).

B. Answer these questions, making use of the idiomatic expressions studied in this lesson.

   1. At what time *is* your lesson *over*?

   2. At what hour *was* the meeting *over* last time?

   3. Do you always arrive at the lesson *on time* or do you sometimes arrive late?

   4. Why did the president have *to put off* his trip to California?

   5. Why is it better never *to put off* until tomorrow what you can do today?

   6. What is the difference in meaning between *to put off* and *to call off?*

   7. Do you *get tired* if you have to walk a long distance?

   8. What do you generally do when you *get hungry?* What do you do when you *get thirsty?* When you *get sleepy?* When you *get tired?* When you *get sick?*

   9. Do you sometimes *get nervous* before an examination or do you have steel nerves?

   10. Where *would* you *rather* go tonight—to the theater or to the opera?

   11. Where *would* you *rather* sit, in the orchestra or in the balcony?

   12. *Would* you *rather* go by bus or by taxi?

   13. Why did the teacher tell William that he *had better* spend more time on his lessons?

   14. Can you give good examples of these idioms in sentences: *to put on, to put off, to put away, to put out?*

**LESSON 8**

1. **to be about to:** (to be at the point of, ready)
   1. I *was* just *about to* leave when you telephoned.
   2. We *were about to* start dinner when Tina arrived.
   3. Have you gone to bed yet? No, but I *was* just *about to*.

2. **to turn around:** (to move in order to face in the opposite direction) (S)
   1. I *turned around* and saw that Gertrude was sitting directly behind me.
   2. The man *turned* the car *around* and drove back the way he came.

3. **to take turns:** (to alternate, not at the same time)
   1. During the trip Gary and I *took turns* driving the car; he would drive for about a hundred miles and then I would drive for about another hundred miles.
   2. Susan and her brother *take turns* doing the dishes; she does them one night and he does them the next night.

4. **to pay attention:** (to give notice or observation to, place importance on) (S)
   1. He never *pays attention* to anything his teacher says, so he frequently doesn't know what's happening.
   2. You will have to *pay* more *attention* in class if you want to get a better grade.

*Doctor, put the puzzle down and pay attention to the surgery!*

5. to go on: (to continue, proceed)
    1. John *went on* reading and paid no attention to any of us.
    2. *"Go on! Go on!"* she said. "Tell me everything that happened."

6. over and over: (repeatedly)
    1. I have told him the same thing *over and over*.
    2. He seems to make the same mistake *over and over* again.

7. to wear out: (to become shabby and useless from wear) (S)
    1. I must buy a new suit. This one is *worn out*.
    2. What do you do with your old clothes when they are *worn out*?
    3. Rough roads *wear* my tires *out*.

8. to throw away: (to discard) (S)
    1. When my clothes are worn out, I generally *throw* them *away*.
    2. Don't *throw* those magazines *away*. I haven't read them yet.

9. to fall in love: (to begin to love)
    1. They *fell in love* when they were in high school. They got married after graduation.
    2. In the movie I saw last night, the hero *falls in love* with the heroine when he first sees her.

10. to go out: (to leave — also to cease burning)
    1. When I telephoned they told me that she had *gone out*.
    2. Have you got a match? This cigar has *gone out*.
    3. The flame *went out* before he had a chance to light the fire.

11. as yet: (up to the present time, as of now)
    1. *As yet* we have not had an answer from him.
    2. He says that she has not telephoned him *as yet*.

12. to have to do with: (to have some connection with)
    1. Does the new vice-president *have* anything *to do with* the work of the export department?
    2. Ralph insists that he *had* nothing *to do with* writing that letter.

**EXERCISES**

**A.** Substitute, in place of the italicized word or words, the corresponding idiomatic expression partially indicated in parentheses.

1. Tara and Ruth *alternated* helping the teacher after school.

   (take _____ )

2. *Up to the present* we have no information about him.

   (as _____ )

3. The police say that he *was not connected* with the crime.

   (have _____ )

4. He had on a pair of shoes which were completely *useless from wear.*

   (wear _____ )

5. He told us the same thing *repeatedly.*

   (over _____ )

6. Why don't you *discard* those old newspapers?

   (throw _____ )

7. I was *at the point of* calling you when your telegram arrived.

   (about _____ )

8. He *continued* talking as though nothing had happened.

   (go _____ )

9. Each time he tried to light his cigar the match *ceased burning.*

   (go _____ )

10. She *began to love* him when she was only a child.

    (fall _____ )

**B.** Answer these questions, making use of the idiomatic expressions studied in this lesson.

1. Why did the driver have *to turn* the car *around?*

2. Whom do you see when you *turn around?*

3. Why do the two boys *take turns* helping in the kitchen each night?

4. Who *took turns* with Carl driving the car on the trip to Florida?

*Congratulations, Higgins. You're in charge of the ship now.*

5. Whom were you *about to* telephone when your friend called?

6. What were you *about to* say when I interrupted you?

7. When your clothes are *worn out*, do you *throw* them *away* or give them to someone?

8. Do you like to keep old magazines or do you always *throw* them *away*?

9. Why did William *throw away* that newspaper?

10. Do you always *pay attention* in class to everything the teacher says?

11. Did Joseph *have* anything *to do with* breaking the window in the school or was he in the clear?

12. Do the students in your school *have* anything *to do with* preparing the school newspaper?

13. Have you ever *fallen in love* with anyone?

14. Why do some people seem to *fall in love* more easily than others?

15. If a cigarette *goes out* while you are smoking it, what must you do?

16. What time did you *go out* last night?

**LESSON 9**

1. **to wake up: (to awaken) (S)**
   1. Marge *woke up* this morning very early but did not get up until about ten o'clock.
   2. I *wake up* at the same time every morning without having to use an alarm clock.
   3. An explosion in the street *woke* us *up*.

2. **to be in charge of: (to manage, be responsible for)**
   1. Jane *is in charge of* the office while Mr. Haig is away.
   2. Who *is in charge of* the arrangements for the dance next week?

3. **as soon as: (just after, when)**
   1. *As soon as* the first snow falls, we put in our winter storm windows.
   2. I'm busy now, but I'll meet you *as soon as* I've finished this job.

4. **to get in touch with: (to communicate with)**
   1. You can *get in touch with* him by calling the Gotham Hotel.
   2. I have been trying all morning *to get in touch with* Miss Peters, but her phone is always busy.

5. **to have a good time: (to enjoy oneself, pass a period of time pleasantly)**
   1. We all *had a good time* at the party last night.
   2. Did you *have a good time* at the dance? I really enjoyed it.

*As soon as you finish with the sports section, I suggest you turn to the "Help Wanted" ads!*

6. to take care of: (to watch, give attention to) (S)
   1. Who will *take care of* your dog while you are away on vacation?
   2. Dr. Anderson says that you should *take* better *care of* yourself.
   3. "Don't worry about a thing," Henry said, "I will *take care of* everything."

7. once in a while: (occasionally, now and then)
   1. I used to see him often, but now he only comes *once in a while*.
   2. *Once in a while* she goes with us to the movies on Saturday night, but not very often.

8. quite a few: (many)
   1. *Quite a few* students were absent yesterday; in fact, more than 40% were not here.
   2. We did not expect many people to attend, but *quite a few* came to the meeting.

9. used to: (indicates an action or habit which continued for some period of time in the past but eventually ended)
   1. I *used to* buy my suits at Macy's. Now I buy them at Barney's.
   2. When I was younger, I *used to* play tennis quite well.

10. to be used to: (to be accustomed to)
    Note: *To be used to* refers to the continuing present; *used to*, as explained above, relates to the past. *Used to* is always followed by a verb; *to be used to* is followed by a noun or a gerund.
    1. He *is used to* this climate and the changes in temperature do not affect him.
    2. I *am used to* studying with Ms. Schwartz and therefore prefer not to change to another teacher.

11. to get used to: (to become used or adjusted to)
    1. You will soon *get used to* this climate and then the changes in temperature will not affect you.
    2. I can't seem *to get used to* wearing glasses.

12. back and forth: (backward and forward)
    1. The lion keeps pacing *back and forth* in its cage.
    2. Why does Grandma keep rocking *back and forth* in her chair?

**A.** Substitute, in place of the italicized word or words, the corresponding idiomatic expression partially indicated in parentheses.

**EXERCISES**

1. I used to meet him *occasionally* on Fifth Avenue.

   (once _____ )

2. Helen has promised *to watch and care for* the baby while we go to the movies.

   (take _____ )

3. *Many* people were injured in the accident.

   (quite _____ )

4. He *formerly played* the violin in a famous orchestra.

   (used _____ )

5. We *enjoyed ourselves* at the picnic.

   (have _____ )

6. I will *communicate* with you as soon as I have any news.

   (get _____ )

7. You will *become accustomed to* his manner of speaking soon.

   (get _____ )

8. Who *is responsible for* that project while Mr. Stein is away?

   (is _____ )

9. The child's swing went *backwards and forwards*.

   (back _____ )

10. What time did you *awaken* this morning?

    (wake _____ )

**B.** Answer these questions, making use of the idiomatic expressions studied in this lesson.

1. How can I *get in touch with* you tomorrow?

2. Why were you unable *to get in touch with* Eliza last night?

3. What time did you *wake up* this morning; what time did you *get up?*

4. Do you have to use an alarm clock in order *to wake up* each morning?

5. Did the thunderstorm *wake* you *up* last night?

6. Who *is in charge of* the cafeteria in your school?

7. Will you call me *as soon as* you finish your homework?

8. Do you like *to take care of* young children?

9. Who *takes care of* preparing the meals and buying the food in your home?

10. Do you go to the movies frequently or only *once in a while?*

11. Do you prepare your lessons every night or only *once in a while?*

12. Did you *have a good time* at the party last Saturday night?

13. Who *used to be* your English teacher before you began to study in your present class?

14. Do you have many relatives? (Use *quite a few*)

# LESSON 10

1. **to make sure:** (to see about something yourself, become sure or certain of)
   1. *Make sure* you turn off the radio before you go out.
   2. He told me *to make sure* to telephone him at exactly 3 o'clock.
   3. I ran to school to *make sure* I got there on time.

2. **now and then:** (occasionally)
   1. I don't see him very often, but *now and then* we have lunch in the same restaurant.
   2. I don't often get sick, but *now and then* I do catch cold.

3. **to get rid of:** (to become free of, escape from)
   1. We can't seem *to get rid of* the mice in our apartment.
   2. It certainly took Mr. Flores a long time *to get rid of* that salesman.

4. **who's who:** (who the different people in a group are)
   1. There are so many dancers on the stage in the same type of costume that it's hard to tell *who's who*.
   2. It was hard for the new teacher to tell *who was who* in our class for the first few days.

5. to go with: (to match, harmonize in color or design) (S)
   1. That bow tie doesn't *go with* that red skirt at all.
   2. Your tan shoes will *go* well *with* that dress.

6. to go with: (to go out together, to keep company with, as in the case of a couple who frequently go out together or have dates)
   1. Andy has been *going with* Eda for about two years; they plan to get married next month.
   2. She *went with* Richard for about six months, but now she has a new boyfriend.

7. to come from: (to originate in—often used to refer to one's home district)
   1. I thought he *came from* Texas but I just learned that he *comes from* New England.
   2. What part of South America does she *come from*? She *comes from* Peru.

8. to make good time: (to travel rapidly at good speed) (S)
   1. We *made* very *good time* on our trip to Florida; it only took 18 hours.
   2. It rained all the time, so we didn't *make good time* driving to New York.

*Harry, would you please get rid of that stupid watch!*

9.  to mix up, to be mixed up, to get mixed up: (to confuse, to be confused, to get confused) (S)
    1. Instead of helping me, his explanation only *mixed* me *up*.
    2. We *got mixed up* in our directions, took the wrong road, and drove many miles out of our way.
    3. The postman *was mixed up*, so he delivered the package to the wrong house.

10. to see about: (to attend to, take care of)
    1. Who is going *to see about* getting us a larger room for this big class? I'm too busy.
    2. The registrar said that he would *see about it*. Do you think at the same time he will *see about* getting permission for us to meet at a different hour?

11. to make out: (to do, succeed)
    1. I did not *make out* very well on my last examination.
    2. How did Raymond *make out* when he went to look for work yesterday?

12. by heart: (by memory)
    1. He knows many passages from Shakespeare *by heart*.
    2. American school children should learn Lincoln's Gettysburg Address *by heart*.

# EXERCISES

A.  Find and underline the expression given in parentheses that corresponds to the italicized idiom.

    1. If I say Dave is *making out* well in his work, I mean that he
       (likes his work, is succeeding, is leaving, is about to begin).

    2. When one *makes good time*, he
       (has a good time, travels at a good speed, is contented).

    3. To learn something *by heart* is to learn it
       (quickly, slowly, well, by memorizing it).

    4. One way of *getting rid of* something is to
       (look at it, admire it, keep it, throw it away).

    5. If Kay's purse *goes* well *with* her dress, then her purse and dress
       (are expensive, are pretty, are worn out, look good together).

6. *Now and then* means
(often, suddenly, early, occasionally).

7. *To make sure of* something is to
(be certain of it, call it off, turn it off).

8. To *come from* is to
(move to, enter, originate in, go to).

9. *To be mixed up* is to be
(happy, worried, confused, late).

10. *To see about* something is to
(attend to it, go to see it, admire it, look at it).

**B.** Answer these questions, making use of the idiomatic expressions studied in this lesson.

1. How did you *make out* in your last English examination?

2. When John went to look for work yesterday, how did he *make out*? Did he fail to get the job or was he hired?

3. What colors *go* well *with* brown? What colors *go* well *with* green?

4. How long has Hank *been going with* Grace?

5. How long did Ellen and Tim *go together* before they *got married*?

6. Do you go to the movies very often or only *now and then*?

7. What is the best way *to get rid of* mice in an apartment?

8. Is it easy or difficult *to get rid of* a foreign accent?

9. Can you tell *who's who* on your favorite TV show?

10. What part of Europe did Charles De Gaulle *come from*?

11. What part of the United States does your English teacher *come from*?

12. Do you ever *get mixed up* when using English idioms?

13. What is the difference between *to have a good time* and *to make good time*?

14. What famous poems or speeches do you know *by heart*?

15. Is it easy or difficult for you to learn things *by heart*?

# REVIEW

LESSONS 1–10

**A.** In the blank spaces at the right, give a ONE-WORD synonym for the italicized word or words. Follow the example in the first sentence.

1. She did not want to *take part* in the meeting.    participate

2. He *called up* all his friends to say good-bye.   _____

3. He *took off* his hat and coat.   _____

4. I'll be back *right away.*   _____

5. Be sure to *put out* the light before you leave.   _____

6. They *got on* the train in Washington.   _____

7. We waited and *at last* he arrived.   _____

8. I was unable to *find out* her name.   _____

9. Her health is improving *little by little.*   _____

10. Last night some friends *called on* us.   _____

11. She lives *by herself* in a furnished room.   _____

12. We *talked over* your problem for a long time.   _____

13. I want to *pick out* a present for my friend.   _____

14. Bert is *getting along* well in his studies.   _____

15. The accident *took place* on Beacon Street.   _____

16. We expect him to *get back* next week.   _____

17. He has *made up his mind* to stay with us.   _____

18. The game was *called off* on account of rain.   _____

19. She has gone back to California *for good*.  _____

20. *All of a sudden* the lights went out.  _____

21. *At times* he does much better work.  _____

22. He *kept on* talking for two hours.  _____

23. The meeting was *put off* until next week.  _____

24. *By the way*, have you seen Carlos recently?  _____

25. We *took turns* driving the car.  _____

26. I have told him the same thing *over and over*.  _____

27. Don't *throw away* those magazines yet.  _____

28. You can *get in touch with* him at his office.  _____

29. I *woke up* very early this morning.  _____

30. He comes here *once in a while*.  _____

31. *As soon as* you finish, call me.  _____

32. I see him *now and then* on Michigan Avenue.  _____

33. These gloves do not *go with* this dress.  _____

34. We got *mixed up* in our directions.  _____

35. He broke the mirror *on purpose*.  _____

**B.** Substitute, in place of the italicized words or phrases, an idiomatic expression with *to get*. (Examples: *get on, get off, get along, get back, get over, get sick, get to a place, get in touch with, get used to, get rid of*, etc.)

1. How is Helen *doing* in her new job?
   (Example: How is Helen *getting along* in her new job?)

2. Mr. Evans will not *return* until next week.

3. You can *communicate with* him by writing to him at the Roosevelt Hotel.

4. We are gradually *becoming accustomed to* this climate.

5. We didn't *arrive in* Washington until almost eight o'clock.

6. We *boarded* the bus at 34th Street.

7. It took him several months to *recover from* the attack of pneumonia.

8. His hat fell in the lake and *became* wet.

C. Substitute, in place of the italicized sections, an idiomatic expression with *to take*. (Examples: *take off, take out, take part in, take a walk, take place, take turns, take care of,* etc.)

1. Gil did not *participate in* our discussion.

2. She *removed* her hat and gloves.

3. He *extracted* a dollar bill from his wallet.

4. Peg and I *alternated* helping the teacher to clean the blackboards.

5. The accident *occurred* on the corner of Fifth Avenue and 23rd Street.

6. Ruth will *watch* the baby while we go to the movies.

D. Substitute, in place of the italicized sections, an idiomatic expression with *to look*. (Examples: *look at, look for, look up, look out, look over*)

1. He is *seeking* the fountain pen which he lost yesterday.

2. You will have to *search for* his number in the telephone book.

3. I will *examine* this and return it to you tomorrow.

4. He stood *watching* me as though he had never seen me before.

E. Make up sentences, oral and written, using the following idioms.

| | | |
|---|---|---|
| to put on | to call up | to make up one's mind. |
| to put off | to call on | |
| to put away | to call off | to make good |

1. to keep out, off, away from, etc.: (to stay out, off, away from) (S)
   1. There was a large sign just outside the door which said: "Danger! *Keep out!*"
   2. *Keep* that dog *out* of this store!
   3. The policeman told the children to *keep off* the grass.
   4. You'd better *keep* your daughter *away from* that dog; he might bite her.

2. to find fault with: (to criticize, complain about something)
   1. It is very easy *to find fault with* the work of others.
   2. He is always *finding fault with* the work of his employees, even though they try to please him.

3. to be up to (one): (to depend upon the decision or responsibility of someone)
   1. It's *up to* you whether we go to the reception or not. It's not *up to* me.
   2. It *is up to* the president to decide how many troops will be sent; no one else has the authority.

4. off and on: (irregularly, occasionally — also on and off)
   1. We don't go to the theater often — just *off and on.*
   2. She comes here *off and on* to see what new books we have.

5. to catch fire: (to begin to burn)
   1. No one seems to know how the building *caught fire.*
   2. Do not stand too close to that stove. Your clothes may *catch fire.*

6. to look into: (to investigate, examine carefully)
   1. The police are *looking into* the past record of the suspect.
   2. The electrician has promised *to look into* our faulty wiring and give us an estimate next week.

7. to take hold of: (to grasp)
   1. The two movers *took hold of* the opposite ends of the table and carried it out easily.
   2. The blind man *took hold of* my arm and I led him across the street.

8. to be out of the question: (to be impossible, unthinkable)
   1. When I asked my brother whether he could go with us on a cruise he said that it *was out of the question* at this time of the year, because he was too busy.
   2. The union thought that management's offer *was out of the question,* so the workers went on strike.

9.  to get through: (to finish)
    1.  I didn't *get through* studying last night until almost eleven o'clock.
    2.  What time does your sister *get through* work every day?

10. all at once: (suddenly, without warning)
    1.  *All at once* the sky became dark and it started to rain.
    2.  We were walking along Fifth Avenue when *all at once* we heard a shot.

11. to keep track of: (to keep or maintain a record of)
    1.  Do you *keep track of* the long distance telephone calls which you make in your office each month?
    2.  We are going to *keep track of* all our expenses while we are in Mexico.

12. to be (get) carried away: (to be greatly affected by a strong feeling) (S)
    1.  They were so patriotic that they *got carried away* and cried every time they heard their country's national anthem.
    2.  I *was carried away* by the romantic movie I saw last night.
    3.  Don't let your anger *carry* you *away*: try to stay calm.

# EXERCISES

A.  Substitute, in place of the italicized word or words, the corresponding idiomatic expression partially indicated in parentheses.

1.  That house is made of a material which *begins to burn* easily.

    (catch _____ )

2.  There were signs everywhere telling people to *remain outside*.

    (keep _____ )

3.  *Suddenly* there was a loud noise and the door flew open.

    (all _____ )

4.  The mayor has promised to *investigate* the public scandal.

    (look _____ )

5.  We see him *occasionally*.

    (off _____ )

6. *It's your responsibility* to get to school on time.

(up _____ )

7. He had to *grasp* the railings to keep from falling.

(take _____ )

8. I *finished* at about eight o'clock.

(get _____ )

9. Such a thing is absolutely *impossible*.

(out of _____ )

10. We must *maintain a record* of all our expenses.

(keep _____ )

11. I hope Jenny doesn't *lose her composure* and cry when she sees me in the hospital.

(get _____ )

12. He seems to enjoy *criticizing* my work.

(find _____ )

B. Answer these questions, making use of the idiomatic expressions studied in this lesson.

1. Why should one always *take hold of* the railing when he goes downstairs?

2. Who *took hold of* your arm as you crossed the street?

3. What time did you *get through* studying last night?

4. What time does your father *get through* work every day?

5. Why do they have so many signs near that weapons factory telling everyone *to keep out?*

6. Why are there so many signs in the park saying: *"Keep off* the grass"?

7. Is it easy to *find fault with* the work of others?

8. Do you watch TV every night or just *off and on?*

9. Do you go to the theater regularly or just *off and on?*

10. Does paper *catch fire* more easily than wood?

11. What other materials *catch fire* easily?

12. Do you *keep track of* the money you spend every day?

13. *Is it up to* you or your parents to decide where you will go tonight?

14. *Is it up to* Henry or his parents to decide which university he will attend?

15. Why did you *get carried away* at the shopping center and spend all your money?

# LESSON 12

1. **up to date:** (timely, modern, brought up to the present time)
   1. This catalogue is not *up to date.* It was published several years ago.
   2. That new structure is one of the most modern and *up-to-date* apartment houses in the city.*

2. **out of date:** (no longer available, current, or in use)
   1. Silent movies have been *out of date* for many years.
   2. She insists on wearing *out-of-date* clothes.*

3. **to blow up:** (to destroy by explosion, to explode) (S)
   1. When the torpedo struck it, the ship immediately *blew up.*
   2. Why did the soldiers *blow up* all the bridges when they retreated?
   3. Did they have to *blow* them all *up?*

4. **to do over:** (to repeat) (S)
   1. The teacher made all of us *do* our exercises *over* because there were so many mistakes in them.
   2. This letter is so badly typed that I think I'd better *do* it *over.*
   3. The violinist *did* that difficult passage *over* and over.

5. **to burn down:** (to burn to the ground) (S)
   1. Their home *burned down* and they had to build a new one.
   2. The fire spread quickly and, before the firemen arrived, the whole block of old buildings had *burned down.*
   3. After that sagging barn collapsed, the farmer *burned* it *down.*

---

*Note how these terms use hyphens when they appear before nouns, but not when they are used as predicate adjectives.

*How's your insurance policy, Everett? Is it up to date?*

6. **to burn up:** (to burn completely) (S)
   1. He *burned* the letter *up* and threw the ashes into the fireplace.
   2. All his books were *burned up* in the fire.

7. **to burn out:** (to stop functioning, become useless — said of electrical equipment) (S)
   1. There are no lights anywhere in the house. Perhaps a fuse has *burned out*.
   2. We need some new electric light bulbs. Both of these bulbs are *burned out*.
   3. If you overload your engine, you will *burn* it *out*.

8. **to make good:** (to succeed)
   1. He is a hard worker, and I am sure that he will *make good* in that new job.
   2. Alma has always *made good* in everything she has done.

9. **it stands to reason:** (to be clear and logical)
   1. *It stands to reason* that if he never prepares his lessons, he is not going to pass this course.
   2. *It stands to reason* that a person without experience cannot do the work as well as an experienced person.

10. **to break out:** (to occur suddenly)
    1. The newspaper says that an epidemic of measles has *broken out* in Chicago this past week.

2. He was living in Iran when the war *broke out*.
3. Every time I eat tomatoes, I *break out* in a rash; I must be allergic to them.

11. as to: (concerning, with reference to)
    1. *As to* the money, we will simply have to borrow some from the bank.
    2. There is no doubt *as to* her intelligence; she's the smartest one in the class.

12. to feel sorry for: (to pity, feel compassion for)
    1. I *feel sorry for* anyone who has to work at night.
    2. I *felt sorry for* Pierre when he broke his foot.

13. to take (something) for granted: (to accept as true without investigation) (S)
    1. He spoke English so well that I *took for granted* that he was an American.
    2. Did you *take* it *for granted* that his check was good? Didn't you ask any questions?
    3. Don't *take* everybody's promises *for granted*.

# EXERCISES

A. Find and underline the expression given in parentheses that corresponds to the italicized word or words.

1. *To blow up* is to
   (extinguish, explode, decrease in size, ache).

2. If a place *burns down*, it
   (burns rapidly, does not burn at all, burns slowly, burns to the ground).

3. *To burn up* is to
   (burn slowly, burn completely, explode, go out).

4. Which of the following can *burn out*
   (a desk, a ship, a fuse, a curtain).

5. If I say that Allan *made good* in his last position, I mean that he
   (always arrived on time, failed, liked it, succeeded).

6. If I say that something *stands to reason*, this means that it is
   (difficult to understand, clear and logical, foolish).

7. *As to that* means

(because of that, in addition to that, concerning that, despite that).

8. *To feel sorry for* someone is to
   (like him, pity him, praise him, hate him).

9. Instead of saying that an epidemic has *happened suddenly,* we generally say that it has
   (stopped, burned out, broken out).

10. *To take* something *for granted* is to
    (permit it, object to it, look it over, accept it without investigation).

**B.** Answer these questions, making use of the idiomatic expressions studied in this lesson.

1. What is the difference between burning something and *burning* something *up?*

2. What is the difference between *to burn up* and *to burn down?*

3. If a building burns to the ground, do we say that it *burned up* or *burned down?*

4. What happens to the lights in your home when a fuse *burns out?*

5. What do you do with electric lights when they *burn out?*

6. Do you prefer things which are *out of date* or those which are *up to date?*

7. Which is the most *up-to-date* department store in your city?

8. Why did you *take* it *for granted* that Mr. Livingston was an American?

9. Did you *take* it *for granted* that the weather would be good today?

10. Why did you *take* it *for granted* that you were going to receive a good mark in English?

11. Why did you have *to do over* the grammar exercises which you prepared last night?

12. Do you like to have *to do* things *over?*

13. Why does his employer feel sure that John will *make good* in his new job?

14. Why does it *stand to reason* that Mary will learn English faster than Juanita?

15. Why does *it stand to reason* that the climate of Panama will be warmer than the climate of Canada?

16. In what year did World War II *break out?*

17. Has an epidemic of influenza ever *broken out* in your country?

# LESSON 13

1. **to break down:** (to stop working — said generally of motors and similar mechanical objects)
    1. Our car *broke down,* so they had to tow it to a garage.
    2. The elevator *broke down,* and we had to walk up to the tenth floor.

2. **to turn out:** (to become or result in)
    1. Although it looked like rain this morning, it has *turned out* to be a fine day.
    2. Julie has *turned out* to be the best student in our English class.

3. **to become of:** (to happen to — said of someone or something missing)
    1. What has *become of* my pencil? I had it ten minutes ago, but now I can't find it.
    2. I wondered what *became of* you. I looked for you for hours, but I couldn't locate you.

4. **to give up:** (to surrender, renounce) (S)
    1. The enemy *gave up* without any resistance.
    2. King Edward VIII *gave up* his throne in order to marry the woman he loved.
    3. Our teacher has tried many times *to give up* smoking, but he can't seem to *give it up.*

5. **to take pity on:** (to pity, feel sympathy for)
    1. Tom's sister *took pity on* him and lent him some money.
    2. It's raining; why don't you *take pity on* me and drive me to school in your car?

6. **to cross out:** (to cancel — by marking with crosses) (S)

1. The teacher *crossed out* several incorrect words in my composition and wrote in the correct ones.
2. Why did you *cross out* the last line of your letter?
3. I *crossed* it *out* because it was repetitious.

7. **to take into account:** (to consider while judging a fact) (S)
   1. You should *take into account* that she has been sick recently. She could do better if she were well.
   2. That sales person never *takes into account* the fact that I am very busy in the mornings.
   3. The judge *took* the prisoner's youth *into account* before sentencing him.

8. **to make clear:** (to explain, clarify) (S)
   1. The teacher *made* my mistake *clear*.
   2. You must *make clear* to him that he should never be rude again.
   3. His explanation *made* the problem *clear* to me.

9. **to take a look at:** (to look at)
   1. *Take a look at* the ring Jessica is wearing today; it's beautiful.
   2. She *took* one *look at* the silly kittens and began to laugh.

10. **to have on:** (to be wearing) (S)
    1. How do you like the hat which Grace *has on* today?
    2. When I went into the room, he *had* nothing *on* except his shorts.

11. **to come to:** (to revive, regain consciousness)
    1. She fainted and did not *come to* for at least half an hour.
    2. At first they thought the man was dead, but soon he *came to*.

12. **to call for:** (to come to an office, home, store, etc., in order to get someone or something, to require)
    1. He promised *to call for* me at my home at 7 o'clock.
    2. This recipe *calls for* some baking soda, but we don't have any.

# EXERCISES

**A.** Substitute, in place of the italicized word or words, the corresponding idiomatic expression partially indicated in parentheses.

1. This group has *become* the best class in the school.

   (turn _____ )

2. What has *happened to* my new notebook?

   (become _____ )

3. It was difficult for him to *stop the habit of* smoking.

   (give _____ )

4. The judge seemed to *feel sorry for* the old man and gave him a light sentence.

   (take _____ )

5. You must *consider* the fact that he has had little education.

   (take _____ )

6. *Look at* the woman who is sitting across from us.

   (take _____ )

7. It was almost a half hour before she *revived*.

   (come _____ )

8. She *canceled with crosses* two of the answers on my examination paper.

   (cross _____ )

9. We will *come to pick you up* at eight o'clock.

   (call _____ )

10. Their automobile *stopped working* and John had to walk six miles to the nearest garage.

    (break _____ )

**B.** Answer these questions, making use in your answers of the idiomatic expressions studied in this lesson.

1. What color shoes does Laura *have on* today?

2. What is the size of the sweater Alex *has on* today?

3. Who has *turned out* to be the best student in your English class?

4. Has the weather this month *turned out* to be warm or cold?

5.  Has the study of English idioms *turned out* to be interesting or dull for you?

6.  Is it easy or difficult for a person *to give up* smoking?

7.  Why is George going *to give up* studying English?

8.  Did you *take pity on* that old man who asked you for money? Why?

9.  Why did Esther *take pity on* that stray cat and let it come into her house?

10. When someone faints, what should you do in order to help him or her *come to?*

11. When someone you knew fainted, how long was it before he or she *came to?*

12. What did the doctor do to make the unconscious person *come to?*

13. What time are your friends going to *call for* you tonight?

14. Is tennis a sport which *calls for* much physical strength?

15. What facts should we *take into account* when we judge Juan's progress in English?

16. Can you give good examples of these idioms in sentences: *to call up, to call down, to call on, to call off, to call for?*

# LESSON 14

1.  to eat in — to eat out: (*to eat in* means to eat at home; *to eat out* means to eat in a restaurant)
    1.  We *ate in* last night but tonight we are going *to eat out* at Gino's.
    2.  When you *eat out*, what restaurant do you generally go to?

2.  to play tricks on: (to make someone the victim of a trick or joke)
    1.  The older boys are always *playing tricks on* Carl. They hide his hat, steal his books, etc.
    2.  They tried *to play a trick on* the professor but she was too clever for them.

3. **to look after:** (to watch over, take care of)
   1. Grandma will *look after* the baby while we go to the lecture.
   2. Who is going *to look after* your house plants while you are away?

4. **to feel like:** (to be inclined, have the desire to)
   1. I don't *feel like* studying tonight. Let's go to a hockey game.
   2. I *feel like* taking a long walk. Would you like to go with me?

5. **once and for all:** (in a final manner, definitively)
   1. My daughter told her boyfriend *once and for all* that she wouldn't go out with him any more.
   2. She said that he should stop telephoning her late at night, *once and for all*.
   3. *For once and for all*, I can't go with you, so stop asking me.

6. **to hear from:** (to receive news from)
   1. Do you *hear from* Ed often? No, he hasn't written.
   2. His parents are worried because they haven't *heard from* him in more than two months.

*I think we'll have a job opening for you in a minute, Mr. Collins, if you feel like waiting.*

7. to hear of: (to know about, to hear mention of)
   1. When I asked directions, the police officer said she had never *heard of* any street by that name.
   2. She rejected my proposal strongly, saying, "I won't *hear of* it!"

8. to make fun of: (to laugh at, joke about)
   1. They are *making fun of* Carla's new hair style; it's strange.
   2. Don't *make fun of* Luis' English. He is doing the best he can.

9. to come true: (to prove to be true or correct)
   1. What the newspaper said about the weather for today has certainly *come true*.
   2. Everything the economists predicted about the cost of living has *come true*.

10. as a matter of fact: (in fact, really)
    1. Hans thinks he knows English well but, *as a matter of fact*, he speaks very poorly.
    2. You think that I prefer Barbados to Florida, but *as a matter of fact*, I don't.

11. to have (one's) way — to get (one's) own way: (to do or obtain what one wishes, especially against opposition or contrary advice)
    1. If Henry doesn't *get* his *own way,* he becomes very angry.
    2. My brother always wants to *have* his *own way*, but this time our parents said we could do what I wanted.

12. to look forward to: (to expect, anticipate, usually pleasantly)
    1. We are *looking forward to* Christmas with great pleasure and excitement.
    2. Margaret complains that she has nothing *to look forward to* except the same monotonous work every day.

# EXERCISES

**A.** Find and underline the expression corresponding to the italicized idiom above.

1. If I *look after* someone, I
    (a) follow him everywhere.
    (b) take care of him.
    (c) call on him.

2. If I *feel like doing* something, I
    (a) have the desire to do it.
    (b) feel well.
    (c) feel foolish.

3. If you *hear from* someone, you
    (a) hear about her.
    (b) receive some communication from her.
    (c) listen to her.

4. If you *make fun of* someone, you
    (a) laugh at or ridicule him.
    (b) call him down.
    (c) tell him a joke.

5. If someone *has* her *own way*, she
    (a) loses her way.
    (b) is on the way.
    (c) gets what she wishes.

6. If I *look forward to* something, I
    (a) look it over.
    (b) anticipate it.
    (c) have my eyes straight ahead.

7. If I *eat in* every night, I
    (a) eat a lot.
    (b) eat in a restaurant.
    (c) eat at home.

8. If a prediction *comes true*, it
    (a) turns out to be correct.
    (b) is false.
    (c) turns out to be foolish.

9. If I *play tricks on* someone, I
    (a) laugh and joke with him.
    (b) call him up.
    (c) make him the victim of my jokes.

10. If I tell you something *once and for all*, I tell you
    (a) several times.

(b) in a final and definite manner.

(c) with the hope of pleasing you.

**B.** Answer these questions, making use of the idiomatic expressions studied in this lesson.

1. Have you ever *heard of* the famous English novelist Charles Dickens?

2. What famous English poets have you *heard of?*

3. What famous English dramatists have you *heard of?*

4. How long has it been since you *heard from* home?

5. When was the last time you *heard from* a friend in your country?

6. Do you like *to play tricks* on other people?

7. How do you like it when other people *play tricks on* you?

8. Do you *eat out* every night or do you generally have dinner at home?

9. What are some advantages of *eating out?*

10. What are some advantages of *eating in?*

11. Do you sometimes *make fun of* other people or of other people's things?

12. Do you like it when other people *make fun of* you?

13. Why don't you *feel like* studying tonight?

14. What do you *feel like* doing?

15. Why do some children always have *to have* their *own way?*

16. Do you believe in *giving children their own way?*

17. When you were a child, did you always *have* your *own way?*

18. What event in the near future are you *looking forward to* with great pleasure?

# LESSON 15

1. **inside out—upside down:** (*Inside out* means in a reverse position, with the inner side turned toward the outside; *upside down* means in a reverse position with the upper side turned toward the lower side.)
   1. The wind blew Mom's umbrella *inside out* and ruined it.
   2. For some reason Paul had put his sweater on *inside out;* we could even see the labels.
   3. After the accident both cars lay in the street *upside down* with their wheels spinning in the air.

2. **to fill in:** (to supply what is missing) (S)
   1. We had to *fill in* the blanks on the test.
   2. *Fill in* your name and number on the application.
   3. Sarah wasn't here yesterday so I had to *fill* her *in* on what happened.

3. **to fill out:** (to complete—said of forms, etc.) (S)
   1. Every prospective employee must *fill out* an application giving name, address, previous position, etc.
   2. When she applied for her passport, Grace had *to fill out*

a half dozen different forms and had some difficulty in *filling* them *out*.

4. **to take advantage of:** (to use an opportunity, also to impose upon or to profit at the expense of another person)
   1. I *took advantage of* the special sale and bought a half dozen new shirts.
   2. He *took advantage of* their hospitality and stayed a whole month without paying them anything.

5. **no matter:** (regardless of)
   1. *No matter* how much money he spends on his clothes, he never looks well dressed.
   2. *No matter* where that escaped convict tries to hide, the police will find him.

6. **to take up:** (begin to do or study) (S)
   1. Peg wants *to take up* ceramics when she retires.
   2. If you want to study dentistry, why don't you *take* it *up*?

7. **to take (something) up with (someone):** (to consult— generally with someone higher in position or authority) (S)
   1. I cannot explain the new tax to you. This is something which you will have *to take up with* an accountant.
   2. If we want to have a student dance in the school, we will have *to take* it *up* first *with* the principal.

8. **to take after:** (to resemble a parent or close relative)
   1. With her light hair and blue eyes she seems *to take after* her mother, but in her character she is more like her father.
   2. Which of your parents do you *take after*?

9. **in the long run:** (finally, after a long period of time)
   1. *In the long run*, this synthetic weave will wear better than the woolen one.
   2. You will find that if you work hard at marriage, *in the long run*, your spouse will turn out to be your best friend.

10. **out of:** (Note the following useful and special expressions with *out of*. The usual meaning is *away from* a place or condition)
    1. Helen Phillips and I have been *out of touch* for years. As a matter of fact, we haven't seen each other since high school.

2. This telephone is *out of order*. Use the other one.
3. She was *out of town* for a few days. I think she was in Boston.
4. That store is going *out of business*. They're selling their entire stock.
5. The plane soared *out of sight*.
6. The poor guy went *out of his mind* and so was put in a psychiatric hospital.
7. This piano is *out of tune*. It sounds terrible.
8. I'm afraid that we are almost *out of gas*. Let's stop at that filling station.
9. He has been *out of work* for a long time. I hope he finds a job soon.

11. to run out of: (to exhaust the supply of)
    1. The soldiers *ran out of* ammunition and had to withdraw.
    2. We *ran out of* gas right in the middle of the main street and blocked traffic.

# EXERCISES

A. Substitute, in place of the italicized word or words, the corresponding idiomatic expression partially indicated in parentheses.

1. The man finally went *insane*.

   (out of _____ )

2. He *exhausted his supply* of money and had to return home.

   (run _____ )

3. She had one glove on *with the inside turned toward the outside*.

   (inside _____ )

4. The plates were placed on the table *with the upper side turned toward the bottom*.

   (upside _____ )

5. Both brothers have been *without work* for months.

   (out of _____ )

6. *Regardless of* how often I correct her, she always makes the same mistake.

   (no _____ )

7. What career do you plan *to undertake* after college?

   (take _____ )

8. Our personnel office asked me *to complete* one of their application forms.

   (fill _____ )

9. I had to write down my name, address, and date of birth.

   (fill _____ )

10. Divorce is a matter which you must *consult a lawyer about*.

    (take _____ )

**B.** Answer these questions, making use of the idiomatic expressions studied in this lesson.

1. With her great interest in sports whom does Joyce *take after?*

2. Which one of your grandparents do you *take after?*

3. Where were your friends going when they *ran out of* gas?

4. Why did that gambler *run out of* money so soon on his trip to Atlantic City?

5. What subject is your friend *taking up* in college?

6. Why don't John's parents want him *to take up* medicine?

7. What is the difference between *filling* something *in* and *filling* something *out?*

8. What different forms did you have *to fill out* when you first came to this school?

9. Has the wind ever blown your umbrella *inside out?*

10. Why did the thieves turn everything in the room *upside down?*

11. Why does that salesman go *out of town* so often?

12. In what way did Dorothy *take advantage of* her friend's generosity?

13. Why is that firm going *out of business?*

14. For how long has your friend been *out of work?*

15. Give good examples of the following idioms in sentences: *to take place, to take part in, to take care of, to take into account, to take turns, to take hold of, to take pity on, to take up, to take something up with, to take after.*

# LESSON 16

1. every so often—every now and then: (occasionally)
   1. *Every so often* he and I go to a ball game together.
   2. *Every now and then* we go to Buffalo to visit my relatives there.—usually about three times a year.
2. to get along with: (to live or work harmoniously with)
   1. The proprietor of that men's store *gets along* well *with* all his employees.; he really seems to like them.
   2. Mr. and Mrs. Jones do not *get along with* each other well. They quarrel constantly.
3. hard of hearing: (partially deaf)
   1. You will have to speak a little louder. Ms. Evans is *hard of hearing*.
   2. Please don't shout. I'm not *hard of hearing*.
4. to let go: (to release) (S)
   1. As soon as the officer *let* him *go*, the thief ran away.
   2. Don't *let go* of my hand until we cross the steet.
5. to keep in mind—to bear in mind: (not to forget, remember) (S)
   1. Please *keep in mind* that you promised to call your patient at two o'clock.
   2. "You should *bear in mind* that Lisa is not as strong as she used to be." "O.K., I'll *keep* it *in mind*."
6. to run over; (to strike or pass over with a moving vehicle)
   1. Why doesn't he drive more carefully? He almost *ran over* that child.
   2. The man was *run over* by a train and killed.
7. to keep an eye on: (to watch, guard carefully)
   1. *Keep an eye on* my suitcase while I buy my ticket.
   2. Our neighbor is going *to keep an eye on* our apartment while we are away.

8. to go off: (a. to explode; b. to leave suddenly)
   a. 1. Those firecrackers usually *go off* with a bang.
      2. The gun *went off* while he was cleaning it; it really frightened him.
   b. Vince *went off* without saying good-bye to anyone.

9. to grow out of: (to outgrow, become too large and mature for)
   1. He has a habit of biting his fingernails, but I think he will *grow out of* it.
   2. As a child she used to stutter, but she *grew out of* it.

10. to make the best of: (to accept a bad situation cheerfully and to do the best that one can under the circumstances)
    1. If we cannot find a larger apartment, we will continue living here and simply *make the best of* it.
    2. They have had bad luck, but they always *make the best of* everything by not getting depressed about it.

11. to cut off: (to shorten by cutting the ends—also to terminate abruptly) (S)
    1. The rope was two feet longer than we needed, so we *cut off* the extra length.
    2. In the middle of our telephone conversation we were suddenly *cut off*.
    3. The storm *cut* our electricity *off* for several hours.

12. to cut out: (a. to remove by cutting; b. to stop doing something) (S)
    a. The child likes to *cut out* pictures from the newspaper.
    b. 1. I wish I could *cut out* smoking.
       2. He kept bothering her so finally she told him to *cut* it *out*.

A. Find and underline the expression given in parentheses that corresponds to the italicized idiom.

**EXERCISES**

1. If I *keep an eye on* something, I (like it, see it, watch it, put it away).

2. If a bomb *goes off*, it (fails, explodes, strikes).

3. A person can be *run over* by (a dog, a doctor, a moving vehicle, bomb).

4. *To cut out* something, we generally use a
   (rope, pencil, box, knife).

5. We might say "We have been *cut off*" when we are
   (struck by a car, using the telephone, using scissors).

6. Someone who is *hard of hearing* is
   (difficult to hear, difficult to understand, lazy, deaf).

7. *Every now and then* means
   (sometimes, often, never, seldom).

8. *To let go* of something is to
   (lose it, bring it, need it, release it).

9. *To bear in mind* is to
   (memorize, remember, forget, be lazy).

10. If I *get along with* someone, I
    (know her well, dislike her, live or work harmoniously with her).

**B.** Answer these questions, making use of the idiomatic expressions studied in this lesson.

1. Why was the electricity in your city *cut off* for several hours one day last summer?

2. What do you do if, while talking on the telephone, you are *cut off?*

3. Is it easy or difficult for people *to cut out* smoking?

4. If a person says to you "*Cut it out!*", what does he mean?

5. As a child did you like *to cut out* pictures from the newspapers or magazines?

6. Why did you ask your friend *to keep an eye on* your house while you went on vacation?

7. Do you *get along* well with the other students in your class?

8. Are there certain persons with whom you cannot *get along?* What are they like?

9. Are you the type of person with whom it is easy or difficult *to get along?*

10. For how long has your grandfather been *hard of hearing?*

11. Do you often visit your friends or only *every now and then?*

12. Why did the parent say to the child. "Don't *let go of* my hand" while they crossed the street?

13. Name one or more habits that you had as a child which you later *grew out of?*

14. How did the bus driver happen *to run over* that dog, did his brakes fail or was he negligent?

---

## LESSON 17

1. to blow out: (to explode, go flat—said generally of tires)
    1. On our trip to Florida one of our tires *blew out* but luckily we had a spare in the trunk.
    2. If a tire *blows out* while one is driving at high speed, it can be very dangerous.

2. to shut off: (to stop something which runs, such as water, gas, electrical current, etc.—similar to *turn off*) (S)
    1. Please *shut off* that faucet. If you don't *shut it off*, you'll waste water.
    2. After the storm the electricity was *shut off* for several hours.

3. to shut up: (to close—also to be quiet, stop talking) (Used as a command, *shut up* is rude). (S)
    1. They have *shut up* their town house and have gone to the country for the summer.
    2. She told him *to shut up* and not to say anything more about it.

4. have got: (to have, to possess) (S)
    1. Curtis *has got* a bad cold.
    2. Who*'s got* my fountain pen?
    3. *Have* you *got* a match?
    4. How much money *have* you *got* with you?

5. have got to (do something): (have to do something, must)
    1. I*'ve got to be* back by two o'clock.
    2. He *has got to* go to Chicago tonight.
    3. We*'ve got to* see her today.

6. to keep up with: (to maintain the same speed as)
    1. Frieda works so fast that no one in the office can *keep up with* her.

2. You'll have to walk more slowly. I can't *keep up with* you.

7. **to tell time:** (to be able to know the hour by looking at a watch or clock)
   1. That three-year-old is too young to be able to *tell time.*
   2. At the age of four William was able *to tell time.*

8. **to turn down:** (to reduce in brightness or volume; to reject) (S)
   1. Please *turn down* the radio. It is too loud.
   2. His application for a position with that company was *turned down* because he had no experience.
   3. Laverne tried to join the Navy but was *turned down* because of her bad eyesight.

9. **fifty-fifty:** (divided or split in two equal portions)
   1. Let's share this pizza *fifty-fifty,* half for you and half for me.
   2. Your candidate has a *fifty-fifty* chance of winning the election. Her chances of winning or losing are about the same.

*There's a good chance he'll turn down the insanity plea.*

10. to break in: (to adjust through usage something which is new and stiff; to train a new employee) (S)
    1. These new shoes are hurting me. I'll be glad when they're *broken in*.
    2. It is better to *break* a new car *in* slowly by driving at moderate speeds for the first 500 miles.
    3. After a few weeks, when our new treasurer is *broken in*, she will be very valuable to us.

11. to break into: (to enter by force)
    1. Thieves *broke into* our apartment last night.
    2. They had no trouble *breaking into* the bank, but when they came out, the police were waiting for them.

12. above all: (mainly, especially)
    1. *Above all*, don't mention this to Gerald; he's the last person we can tell.
    2. He does well in all his subjects, *above all*, in mathematics. His math scores are always perfect.

A. Find and underline the expression corresponding to the italicized idiom above.

**EXERCISES**

1. If I*'ve got to* leave early, I
    (a) want to leave early.
    (b) can't leave early.
    (c) must leave early.

2. If someone tells you to *shut up*, he wants you to
    (a) close the door.
    (b) turn off the radio.
    (c) stop talking.

3. If I cannot *keep up with* you, I cannot
    (a) go as fast as you.
    (b) turn off the radio.
    (c) keep my promise.

4. If someone *breaks into* your home, he or she
    (a) visits you.
    (b) leaves a message for you.
    (c) enters by force.

5. If a tire *blows out*, it
    (a) inflates.

    (b) explodes and then goes flat.
    (c) turns off.

6. If someone is *turned down*, she is
    (a) accepted.
    (b) rejected.
    (c) called on.

7. When you *shut* something *off*, you
    (a) turn it off.
    (b) turn it down.
    (c) put it away.

8. We *break in* only those things which are
    (a) old and worn.
    (b) worn out.
    (c) new and stiff.

9. *"Have* you *got* a cigarette?" means
    (a) "Do you smoke cigarettes?"
    (b) "Did you see a cigarette?"
    (c) "Do you have a cigarette to give me?"

10. *To tell time* is to
    (a) count the days.
    (b) look at a clock and know what time it is.
    (c) look at your watch.

11. If a team has a *fifty-fifty* chance of winning a game, then its chances of winning or losing are:
    (a) equal
    (b) unequal
    (c) indifferent

**B.** Answer these questions, making use of the idiomatic expressions studied in this lesson.

1. How old were you when you learned *to tell time?*

2. At what age do children generally learn *to tell time?*

3. When you tell someone *to shut up*, are you using a polite form?

4. *Have* you *got* much homework to do tonight?

5. Where *have* you *got to* go today after the lesson?

6. Why *has* that housewife *got to* go to the supermarket tomorrow?

7. Which student in your class *has got* the largest speaking vocabulary?

8. *Has* the same student *got* the largest reading vocabulary?

9. Why was George *turned down* when he tried to join the Army?

10. When you were young, did you and your sister (brother) always share your toys *fifty-fifty*?

11. In your country, do husbands and wives share all property *fifty-fifty*?

12. What may happen if you are driving a car at high speed and a tire *blows out*?

13. What is the difference between a puncture and a *blow-out*?

14. Why is it difficult for a shorter person *to keep up with* John when they are walking together?

15. Have thieves ever *broken into* your home or apartment?

# LESSON 18

1. to do or go without: (to get along without, to forego)
    1. With prices so high I will have to *do without* a new suit this year.
    2. As a traveling saleswoman, she can't *go without* a car.

2. to watch out for: (to look out for, guard against) (Compare p.16, #1)
    1. There was a sign near the road saying, "Watch Out For Falling Rocks!"
    2. One thief went inside while the other waited outside and *watched out for* the police.

3. to be bound to: (be certain to, sure to)
    1. We *are bound to* be late if you don't hurry.
    2. With business improving they *are bound to* make money this year.

4. for sure: (for certain, without doubt)
    1. In the dark I couldn't tell *for sure* whether it was Polly or Sara.
    2. Do you know *for sure* whether Gene will move back to Washington? No, I'm not certain.

3. It certainly has rained a lot this week. That's *for sure!*

5. to take (someone) for: (to mistake a person for someone else)
   1. With his strong, muscular body, I *took* him *for* an athlete.
   2. What do you *take* me *for*—a fool?

6. to try out: (to test, use during a trial period) (S)
   1. They let me *try out* the sewing machine for several days before buying it.
   2. The government is *trying out* various new types of computers.
   3. Before I purchase that car, I'd like *to try* it *out*.

7. to tear down: (to demolish) (S)
   1. They *tore down* the old building and built a new one.
   2. In order to build the highway, the contractors had *to tear down* a whole block of buildings.
   3. New York is constantly changing. They are always *tearing* something else *down*.

8. to tear up: (to tear completely into small pieces) (S)
   1. She *tore up* the letter angrily and threw it piece by piece into the waste basket.
   2. He told the lawyer *to tear up* the old contract and to prepare a new one.

9. to cut up—to break up—to chop up—to chew up, etc.
   (These forms are similar to *tear up*, explained above. They all suggest an action of cutting, breaking, or chopping something completely into many small pieces.) (S)
   1. The butcher *cut* the meat *up* and then weighed it.
   2. He *broke up* the candy and gave each child a piece.
   3. He *chopped up* the wood into small pieces of about six inches each.
   4. The dog *chewed up* my daughter's doll.

10. to eat up—to clean up—to dress up—to tie up, etc.
    (These forms are also similar to *tear up*, described above. The particle *up* placed after a verb generally suggests an action which is *complete*. Thus to *eat up* something is to eat all of it. *To clean up* is to clean thoroughly and completely, etc.) (S)
    1. After playing all afternoon, we were so hungry that we *ate up* all the cookies in the house.
    2. When you're finished, please *clean up* this mess.
    3. Where is Elsie going all *dressed up?*
    4. The thieves *tied up* the watchman.

**A.** Substitute, in place of the italicized word or words, the idiomatic expression partially indicated in parentheses.

**EXERCISES**

1. With taxes so high I will have to *get along without* a new car this year.

   (do _____ )

2. When you cross the street, be careful and *be on the alert* for traffic.

   (watch _____ )

3. Edna is *certain to* succeed in that busines.

   (bound _____ )

4. I *made a mistake and thought that he was* a Brazilian.

   (take _____ )

5. They will *test* several machines and select the best one.

   (try _____ )

6. He *tore the telegram into small pieces* and threw it away.

   (tear _____ )

7. They *are demolishing* many old buildings in order to build new ones.

   (tear _____ )

8. You can *break that* chalk *into small pieces* with your hand.

   (break _____ )

9. I need rope *to bind* these newspapers together.

   (tie _____ )

10. Marie is *dressed entirely* in her best clothes. She must be going to a party.

    (dress _____ )

**B.** Answer these questions, making use in your answers of the idiomatic expressions studied in this lesson.

1. Do you know *for sure* what you'll do when you finish school?

2. Would you like to *try out* a new Cadillac?

3. Why do you say that Edith is *bound to* get the highest mark in the class?

4. Why is that lazy student *bound to* fail the examination?

5. Why did you *take* that stranger *for* a Cuban?

6. Why does everyone always *take* Olga *for* an Italian?

7. Why are they *tearing down* that building across the street?

8. What is the difference between *to tear something down* and *to tear something up*.

9. What is the difference between *to tear something* and *to tear something up*?

10. What is the difference between *to break down* and *to break something up*?

11. If someone tells you *to watch out for* something, what should you do?

12. What is the difference between *being dressed* and *being dressed up*?

13. If you place the particle *up* after a verb, what meaning does this generally give to the verb?

14. What do we mean when we say that the street is all *torn up*?

# LESSON 19

1. to cut off, tear off, break off, bite off, chew off, etc. (Note: these expressions are used in a literal sense with the meaning of *to remove a piece or section of something* by cutting, tearing, breaking, etc.) (S)
   1. He is *cutting off* the lower branches of the tree. He is using a power saw to *cut* them *off*.
   2. She *tore off* a piece of the paper and gave it to me.
   3. He *broke off* a small piece of candy and gave it to the child.
   4. The lion *bit off* the end of the stick I was holding.

2. to tell (two things or two people) apart — to tell one from the other: (to distinguish between)
   1. The two brothers look so much alike that no one can *tell* them *apart*.
   2. The two coins looked so much alike that it was difficult *to tell one from the other*.

3. all in all: (everything being taken into account, considered in summary)

1. A few things went wrong, but *all in all* it was a good meeting.
2. Leonard got a low grade in one subject, but *all in all* he's a pretty good student.

4. to pass out: (to lose consciousness; also, to distribute)
   1. Richie started to get out of bed, but he was still so weak from his illness that he *passed out* on the floor.
   2. The bartender explained that the customer had just drunk her fifth martini when she *passed out*.
   3. Please help me *pass out* these test papers; each student should get one.

5. to go around: (be sufficient for everyone)
   1. If there aren't enough chairs *to go around*, I can bring some from the other room.
   2. So many people came that there were not enough sandwiches *to go around*.

6. in the (one's) way: (blocking or obstructing, thus causing inconvenience)
   1. He tried to help us but was simply *in the way*.
   2. Is this chair *in your way*? If it is, I'll move it.

7. to put on (weight): (to gain weight, become heavier) (S)
   1. Bob has *put on* a lot of *weight* recently. He's been eating a lot more.
   2. I *put on* at least ten pounds during my vacation. Three big meals a day helped *to put it on*.

*You seem to have put on a little weight, Uncle Trevor.*

8. to put up: (to construct, erect) (S)
   1. The builders are tearing down that old office building in order *to put up* a new one.
   2. They are *putting up* several new buildings in that block.
   3. Some apartments are rented even before the builders *put* them *up*.

9. to put up with: (to tolerate)
   1. I refuse *to put up with* his actions any longer. I'm going to fire him.
   2. How do you *put up with* that noise all day long?

10. in vain: (useless, without result)
    1. All the doctor's efforts were *in vain* and the man finally died.
    2. We tried *in vain* to reach you last night, but your phone was always busy.

11. day in and day out/day after day: (daily, continuously)
    1. *Day after day* he gave the same excuse for his laziness.
    2. *Day in and day out* for a period of six months, he worked on his new novel.

12. to show off: (to display one's ability or possessions in order to attract attention) (S)
    1. Elizabeth swims well but I don't like the way she *shows off* in front of everyone.
    2. Henrietta wants to drive fast simply *to show off* her new car.
    3. Nobody likes him because he is such a *showoff*.
    4. Jonas has a very expensive wristwatch and he never misses an opportunity to *show* it *off*.

# EXERCISES

A. Find and underline the expression given in parentheses that corresponds to the italicized word or words.

   1. If someone is *in* my *way*, he is
      (helping me, going around me, blocking my path).

   2. If there is enough of something *to go around*, this means that there is enough
      (for only a few, for everyone, for those who arrive early).

   3. If a building is being *put up*, it is being
      (torn down, improved, erected).

4. If someone is *displaying his ability or his possessions ostentatiously*, we say that he is
(coming to, eating out, getting rich, showing off).

5. If someone is *putting on* weight, she is
(working hard, weighing something, going on vacation, getting heavier).

6. If I do something *in vain*, I do it
(without interest, without success, hurriedly).

7. If I can't *put up with* something, I can't
(stand it, eat it, admire it, describe it)

8. If I *remove a part of something by tearing it*, I
(tear it down, tear it up, tear it off).

9. If I cannot *tell* you and your sister *apart*, I cannot
(speak to you alone, tell you any secrets, distinguish between you).

10. If someone does something *day in and day out*, he does it
(occasionally, day after day, when the weather is good).

B. Answer these questions, making use of the idiomatic expressions studied in this lesson.

1. Why is it difficult *to tell* Ted and his brother *apart?*

2. In the case of twin brothers or twin sisters, is it always difficult *to tell one* twin *from the other?*

3. I know that it rained part of the time, but *all in all* was your vacation fun?

4. What is the difference between: *the man cut his finger* and *the man cut off his finger?*

5. What is the difference between: *the animal bit the man's hand* and *the animal bit off the man's hand?*

6. What is the difference between: *he tore up a sheet of paper* and *he tore off a sheet of paper?*

7. Why did the movers tell the curious children to get *out of their way?*

8. Why did the teacher ask you whether that chair *was in your way?*

9. Are they *putting up* many new buildings in your town?

10. Which is easier to do: *to tear down* an old building or *to put up* a new one?

11. How does a *show-off* act?

12. Do you like or dislike people who *show off?*

13. Why did the teacher say that she would not *put up with* Diane's absences any longer?

14. Why does Mr. Smith *put up with* so much from his unkind employer?

15. Did you *put on* any weight during your vacation or did you lose weight?

16. Give good examples of these expressions in sentences: *to put on, to put away, to put off, to put out, to put up, to put on* weight.

17. Have you ever been so sick that you *passed out?*

18. Who usually *passes out* the assignment papers in your class?

# LESSON 20

1. to hold still: (to remain quiet — without moving) (S)
   1. How can I take your picture if you don't *hold still?*
   2. *Hold still* a moment while I fix your tie.
   3. If you don't *hold* that camera *still*, you'll get a blurred picture.

2. to know by sight: (to recognize as a result of having seen someone previously) (S)
   1. I have never met our new neighbors; I simply *know* them *by sight*.
   2. Although I have never spoken with either of our two new employees, I *know* them both *by sight*.

3. something the matter — nothing the matter: (something wrong — nothing wrong)
   1. Is there *something the matter* with Rita? She looks pale.
   2. The mechanic says that there is *nothing the matter* with my car now, it's working fine.

4. to bring up: (to rear, raise from childhood; also, to present for attention or consideration) (S)

*McGinley is one of the few employees around here I know by sight.*

1. His mother died when he was young, and his grand-mother *brought* him *up*.
2. She decided against *bringing* the matter *up* at the club meeting.
3. Leslie is moving to Norway because she wants to *bring* her children *up* there.

5. to get lost: (to lose one's direction, become lost)
   1. While driving to Boston, we *got lost* and drove many miles out of our way.
   2. Mick *got lost* in the woods and did not get home until after midnight.

6. to hold up: (a. to rob at the point of a gun; b. to delay) (S)
   a. 1. They *held up* the owner and robbed him of everything.
      2. The thief pointed a gun at Wendy and *held* her *up*.
   b. 1. Shipment of the merchandise was *held up* because of the railroad strike.
      2. Traffic on the bridge was *held up* for several hours because of the accident.

7. to run away: (to leave without notice or permission)

1. He *ran away* from home when he was a child, and never returned.
2. They *ran away* and got married in Boston.
3. My cat is frightened easily; he usually *runs away* from anyone who tries to come near him.

8. to rule out: (to show or say that something cannot be done or considered)
   1. Heather *ruled out* applying to that college in Texas; she wants to go to school in Canada.
   2. The x ray *rules out* the possibility that the bone is broken; your ankle must just be badly sprained.
   3. I wanted to watch TV tonight, but my need to study for a test *rules* that *out*.

9. to see (somebody) off: (to go to a train, ship, or plane in order to say good-bye to someone)
   1. We are going to the airport *to see* Peter *off*. He is going to Europe.
   2. No one went to the station *to see* him *off*, when he left for Cincinnati.

10. to set fire to — to set on fire: (to cause to burn) (S)
    1. No one knows who *set fire to* the building.
    2. Be careful with that match. You will *set* those curtains *on fire*.

# EXERCISES

A. Substitute, in place of the italicized word or words, the idiomatic expression partially indicated in parentheses.

1. Delivery may be *delayed* several weeks because of the flood.

   (hold _____ )

2. Lack of money *makes it impossible* to think about going to college this year.

   (rule _____ )

3. He *left home without permission* when he was eight years old and never returned.

   (run _____ )

4. The same storekeeper has been *robbed at the point of a gun* three times.

   (hold _____ )

5. They *eloped* and got married in Philadelphia.

   (run _____ )

6. If you *lose your direction,* consult your map.

   (get _____ )

7. We went to the station to *say good-bye to John*

   (see _____ )

8. *Remain quiet* a moment while Gloria takes our picture.

   (hold _____ )

9. I have never met him but I *recognize him when I see him.*

   (know _____ )

10. He is an American but he was *raised* in Europe.

    (bring _____ )

B. Answer these questions, making use of the idiomatic expressions studied in this lesson.

   1. Do you know your councilman to speak to or just *by sight?*

   2. Did you ever *run away* from home as a child?

   3. Why do children sometimes *run away* from home?

   4. Have you ever been *held up?*

   5. Do many or few *holdups* take place in the city in which you live?

   6. Why was traffic *held up* on Fifth Avenue for several hours yesterday?

   7. Why was Dot *brought up* by her grandmother instead of by her mother?

   8. How does it happen that Liz was born in the United States but *brought up* in England?

   9. That lady looks very pale. Is there *something the matter* with her?

   10. Have your parents ever *ruled out* something you wanted to do?

   11. Is it difficult *to set fire to* things made of wood?

12. Is it difficult *to set fire to* things made of metal?

13. Have you ever *gotten lost* in the woods or in a strange city? If so, when?

14. What should you do if you *get lost* in a strange city?

15. Do you like to go to the airport *to see* someone *off*?

# LESSON 21

1. **to drive up to—to go up to—to walk up to—to run up to:** (to approach)
   1. We finally *drove up to* a gas station and inquired about the correct route.
   2. She *went up to* him and shook his hand as though she had known him for years.
   3. The child *ran up to* me and began to cry.

2. **to hand in:** (to submit or deliver something that is due) (S)
   1. Every student has *to hand in* an original composition each week.
   2. All the salespeople *hand in* weekly reports.
   3. Are you still working on your term paper, or did you *hand* it *in*?

3. **in case:** (if it happens that; in order to be prepared)
   1. You'd better close your windows *in case* it rains.
   2. Their planes usually leave a little late, but I always get to the airport early, just *in case*.
   3. Cynthia, take your books with you *in case* you have an opportunity to study.

4. **to put together:** (to assemble) (S)
   1. We followed the directions but could not *put* the machine *together*.
   2. After he took the watch apart, he was not able *to put* it *together* again.

5. **to take apart:** (to disassemble, to separate the different parts of an object or mechanism) (S)
   1. It is much easier *to take* a clock *apart* than to put it together again.
   2. In order to fix it, the mechanic had *to take* the carburetor

*apart.*

3. I could never have *taken* it *apart.*

6. **to be better off:** (to be in a more favorable or better condition or situation)
    1. You *will be* much *better off* working in that office than in a factory.
    2. If he is so sick, he *would be better off* in a hospital.

7. **to be well-off:** (to be rich, well-to-do)
    1. They own their own home, have two automobiles, and seem *to be very well-off.*
    2. Her parents *were* once *well-off* but they lost all their money.

8. **to take (someone) by surprise:** (to surprise, to appear unexpectedly)
    1. Her offer *took* me completely *by surprise.*
    2. The president's announcement *took* everyone *by surprise.*

9. **to keep in touch with—to stay in touch with:** (to continue in communication with; see also *to get in touch with,* Lesson 9, No. 4)
    1. You can telephone me every few days, and in that way we can *keep in touch with* each other.
    2. He promised *to stay in touch with* us while he was abroad.

*Either this was put together wrong, Mr. Hill, or I'm taking it apart wrong.*

10. **to be named after:** (to be given the same name as another)
    1. Helen *is named after* her aunt.
    2. My grandson *is named* Calvin, *after* a former president of the United States.

11. **to hold on:** (to keep a tight hold or grip: to pause, wait)
    1. She *held on* to my coat sleeve and refused to let go.
    2. As he began to fall off the ladder, Jane shouted, *"Hold on!"*
    3. *Hold on* a minute! I want to speak to you.
    4. (while telephoning) *Hold on* a minute while I get a pencil and paper.

12. **to think up:** (to invent, discover, find) (S)
    1. I wish I could *think up* a good excuse to give the teacher for my not having prepared my homework.
    2. Every day they *think up* some new trick to play on Doris.
    3. That was a clever idea. Who *thought* it *up?*

# EXERCISES

**A.** Find and underline the expression corresponding to the italicized idiom above.

1. If I *go up to* someone, I
    (a) become angry at her.
    (b) approach her.
    (c) refuse to speak to her.

2. If I *think up* a reason for something, I
    (a) invent it.
    (b) accept it.
    (c) cancel it.

3. *To keep in touch with* someone is to
    (a) keep touching him.
    (b) keep him in sight.
    (c) continue in communication with him.

4. If a person is *well-off*, she is
    (a) poor.
    (b) rich.
    (c) not sick.

5. If I *am named after* someone, I
    (a) have a similar character.
    (b) have been given the same name.
    (c) imitate him in everything.

6. If I *take* something *apart*, I
    (a) criticize it.
    (b) assemble it.
    (c) separate the different parts.

7. If I *put* something *together*, I
    (a) assemble it.
    (b) think it up.
    (c) put it away.

8. If I *hand in* a report, I
    (a) prepare a report.
    (b) submit a report.
    (c) put it away.

9. *To be better off* is to be
    (a) out of town.
    (b) out of work.
    (c) in a better condition than previously.

10. If I say, *"Hold on a moment!"* I mean
    (a) wait.
    (b) this is a robbery.
    (c) call back later.

**B.** Answer these questions, making use of the idiomatic expressions studied in this lesson.

1. How many times a week do the students of your class *hand in* homework to the teacher?

2. Why does Mr. Neal want *to hand in* his resignation to his boss?

3. Which one of her parents *is* Catherine *named after?*

4. *Were you named after* anyone in your family?

5. Which is easier: *to take* a watch *apart* or *to put* it *together* again?

6. Why did the repairman have to *take* the typewriter *apart* in order to repair it?

7. Did the latest eclipse of the sun *take* everyone *by surprise* or did most people expect it?

8. Why did the president's death *take* everyone *by surprise?*

9. What did that man look like who *came up to* you on the street?

10. What is the difference between: *to run up to* someone and *to run over* someone?

11. Why *is* Pat *better off* in her present position than she was in her former one?

12. Why do you say that that patient *would be better off* in a hospital than at home?

13. If we say that someone *is well-off*, do we mean that he is rich or poor?

14. If it is very windy, why do you have *to hold on* to your hat in the street?

15. Why did you tell your friend *to hold on* while you went to get a pencil?

16. What do you carry *in case* of rain?

**LESSONS 1–21**

**A.** In the blank spaces at the right, give a ONE-WORD synonym for the italicized word or words. Follow the example in the first sentence.

1. He *left out* the third question on his examination.                omitted

2. Such a thing is absolutely *out of the question*.

3. We *talked over* the problem for a long time.

4. I didn't *get through* the test until almost eight o'clock.

5. He likes *to find fault with* other people's work.

6. I want *to look over* that letter before it goes out.

7. *All at once* Fran appeared in the doorway.

8. She has always *made good* on every job she has had.

9. He was living in El Salvador when the war *broke out*.  _____

10. The enemy *gave in* without further resistance.  _____

11. She *took pity on* him and gave him some money.  _____

12. You must *take into account* the fact that he was ill.  _____

13. Ida fainted but *came to* immediately.  _____

14. He is planning *to take up* medicine in college.  _____

15. Bella *takes after* her mother in many ways.  _____

16. The poor fellow went *out of his mind*.  _____

17. He is a little *hard of hearing*.  _____

18. Don't *let go of* the rope until I tell you.  _____

19. *Bear in mind* that we must get there before seven.  _____

20. *Keep an eye on* my suitcase while I get my ticket.  _____

21. I wish I could *cut out* smoking.  _____

22. Her application for a passport was *turned down*.  _____

23. They will *try out* the machine tomorrow.  _____

24. They *tore down* the old building and built a new one.  _____

25. All her efforts were *in vain*.  _____

26. They are *putting up* several new buildings there.  _____

27. I refuse to *put up with* his actions any longer.  _____

28. He seems to be *putting on* weight.  _____

29. She was born in Texas but *brought up* in New England. _____

30. That bank has been *held up* several times. _____

B. Substitute, in place of the italicized word or words, an idiomatic expression with *to call*. (Examples: *call up, call on, call for, call off*, etc.)

1. Some friends *visited* us last night.

2. I will *telephone* you at six o'clock.

3. We will *come to pick* you *up* at exactly seven o'clock.

4. The game was *canceled* because of rain.

C. Substitute, in place of the italicized word or words, an idiomatic expression with *to take*. (Examples: *take part in, take off, take out, take place, take turns, take care of, take pity on, take into consideration, take for granted, take advantage of, take up, take up with, take after, take apart*)

1. The accident *occurred* on the corner of Broad and Market Streets.

2. Ben *removed* his hat and coat.

3. I *assumed without investigation* that he was an American.

4. You must *consider* the fact that she was ill at the time.

5. It was much easier to *disassemble* the machine than to put it together again.

6. He plans to *study* law when he goes to college.

7. The meeting will *occur* in Mr. Smith's office.

8. He *exploited* his friend's generosity.

9. You must *consult with Ms. Smith about this*.

10. Patty *resembles* her mother in many ways.

D. Substitute, in place of the italicized word or words, an idiomatic expression with *to make*. (Examples: *make believe, make up one's mind, make sure, make out, make good, make good time, make fun of, make the best of*, etc.)

1. How did you *succeed* in your last English examination?

2. He *pretended* that he was ill.

3. Everyone *laughed and joked about* the dog's little sweater.

4. Our apartment is small but, since we cannot find

anything better, we will have *to do the best that we can under these circumstances.*

5. This letter is so badly written that I cannot *understand* what he means.

6. I am sure that Diane will *succeed* in her new position.

7. In driving to Washington, we *traveled at very good speed.*

8. *Be certain* to get there on time.

E. Substitute, in place of the italicized word or words, an idiomatic expression with *to put.* (Examples: *put off, put out, put up, put away, put up with, put together, put on, put on weight,* etc.)

1. He *extinguished* his cigarette in the ash tray.

2. Harvey seems to be *gaining* weight.

3. They are *erecting* several new buildings in that block.

4. She says she will not *tolerate* his carelessness any longer.

5. The meeting was *postponed* until next week.

6. It is easy to take a watch apart, but it is difficult *to assemble* it again.

F. Give sentences with the following idioms.

| | | |
|---|---|---|
| to get on | to get to a place | to get used to |
| to get off | to get sick, tired, | to get rid of |
| to get along | wet, hungry, etc. | to get through |
| to get back | to get in touch with | to get along with |

G. Give sentences with these idioms.

| | | |
|---|---|---|
| at once | for good | now and then |
| at first | at times | off and on |
| at last | all of a sudden | all at once |
| as usual | once in a while | in the long run |
| so far | quite a few | every so often |

# LESSON 22

1. **to give (someone) a call:** (to telephone) (S)
   1. I'll *give* you *a call* as soon as I get there.
   2. *Give* me a call sometime next week and we'll arrange to have dinner together.

2. **to drop (someone) a line:** (to write briefly to someone) (S)
   1. As soon as I get to Florida, I'll *drop* you *a line*.
   2. If you have time, *drop* me *a line* now and then while you are traveling.
   3. I must *drop a line* to my mother.

3. **to come across:** (to meet or find unexpectedly)
   1. While cleaning the attic yesterday, I *came across* an old photograph of my mother.
   2. I *came across* several interesting facts about Mexico in that book.

*I've never come across anything like it! Only four legs! Two of them don't even reach the ground!*

4. to stand for: (to represent; also, to tolerate)
    1. In this secret code each number *stands for* a letter of the alphabet.
    2. Each stripe in the American flag *stands for* one of the original thirteen colonies; each star *stands for* one of the fifty states.
    3. I don't have *to stand for* such rude behavior.

5. to stand a chance: (to have the possibility)
    1. The New York team *stands a* good *chance* of winning the World Series this year.
    2. Not having had any previous experience, John doesn't *stand a chance* of getting that job.

6. to make faces: (to grimace, assume a facial expression of jest or scorn)
    1. The two quarreling children sat *making faces* at each other.
    2. Stop *making faces* at me; the teacher will catch you.
    3. Instead of being pleased, he *made a face* when I told him the news about my raise.

7. to take pains: (to work carefully and conscientiously)
    1. She *took* great *pains* with her homework because she wanted to get a good grade.
    2. He *takes pains* with everything that he does; he's our most accurate employee.

8. to look up to: (to admire, respect highly)
    1. Our director is a man that everyone *looks up to*; indeed, many of us want to be like him.
    2. Since my daughter started *looking up to* me, I have become more aware of my behavior.

9. to look down on: (to scorn, despise, think of someone as less important)
    1. After Barnes became **go**vernor, those who had called him names and *looked down on* him as a cheap politician regretted their former attitude.
    2. Why should Alma *look down on* him just because his family is poor?

10. to take off: (to leave the ground, said of airplanes)
    1. The plane *took off* at exactly two o'clock.
    2. The accident occurred while the plane was *taking off*.

11. to pull off: (to do something difficult, especially if it requires a special skill) (S)

1. The lawyers *pulled off* something that no one thought they could. They got the two sides to agree to a compromise.
2. She tried several times to beat the world's 100-meter swimming record, and finally she was able to *pull* it *off*.

12. to keep good time: (to run accurately, said of watches and clocks)
    1. Although it is a cheap one, this watch *keeps* very *good time*.
    2. This clock *keeps perfect time*. It's never fast or slow.

# EXERCISES

A. Find and underline the expression given in parentheses that corresponds to the italicized idiom.

1. *To come across* someone is to
   (argue with him, meet him unexpectedly, call him up).
2. *To give* someone *a call* is to
   (telephone her, yell at her, admire her, find her).
3. If I say that I will not *stand for* something, I mean that I will not
   (pay for it, look it over, tolerate it).
4. *To drop* someone *a line* is to
   (throw him a rope, send him a telegram, write him a letter).
5. If I *take pains* with something, I
   (hurt myself, enjoy doing it, do it very carefully).
6. *To look up to* someone is to
   (be shorter than she, respect her highly, search for her).
7. When a plane *takes off*, it
   (arrives, explodes, leaves the ground).
8. If something *stands a chance*, it
   (can't succeed, remains upright, might succeed).
9. If a watch *keeps good time*, it
   (runs fast, needs winding, often stops, runs accurately).
10. *To look down on* someone is to
    (be taller than he, overlook him, treat him with scorn).

**B.** Answer these questions, making use of the idiomatic expressions studied in this lesson.

1. Why doesn't Michael *stand a chance* of passing his English examination?

2. Why doesn't Frank *stand a chance* of winning the tennis match?

3. In the American flag, what does each one of the stripes *stand for*?

4. What does your middle initial *stand for*?

5. What do the letters Ph.D. after Dr. Crescy's name *stand for*?

6. Who did you *come across* on Broadway last week?

7. What slight difference in meaning is there between *to meet someone* and *to come across someone*?

8. Why did everyone *look up to* Gen. Chapman after his return from the war?

9. Why is it wrong *to look down on* those who are less fortunate than ourselves?

10. Why does that bright student *look down on* the other students in his class?

11. If I *take pains* in doing something, do I do it carefully or carelessly?

12. How did your team *pull off* its latest victory?

13. Does your watch *keep good time* or does it sometimes run fast or run slow?

14. Did the accident occur while the plane was landing or while it was *taking off*?

# LESSON 23

1. to make do: (to manage with a substitute which is less than desired)
   1. Pearl did not have a clean shirt so she had *to make do* with the one she wore yesterday.
   2. In these economic hard times, we all have *to make do* with less.
   3. This typewriter isn't exactly what I wanted, but I suppose I'll just have *to make do*.

2. to give birth to: (to bear, bring forth children)
   1. Jane's mother has just *given birth to* twins.
   2. Yesterday our daughter-in-law *gave birth to* a six-pound baby boy.

3. to taste of: (to have the same flavor as)
   1. This omelet *tastes of* onions. Did you put any in?
   2. If you don't cover that dish, everything in the refrigerator will *taste of* cabbage.

4. to get on (one's) nerves: (to make one nervous, be annoyed)
   1. I wish they would turn off that radio. It's *getting on* my *nerves*.
   2. She talks so much that she *gets on* my *nerves*.

5. to put down: (to suppress, quell) (S)
   1. The troops easily *put down* the rebellion.
   2. They had to call the police in order *to put down* the riot.
   3. There was a threatening demonstration in the park, but the police *put it down*.

6. to go in for: (to have as an interest or hobby, to dedicate oneself to)
   1. Hal *goes in for* tennis while his wife *goes in for* painting and sculpture.
   2. What sports do you *go in for*?

7. to stay up: (to remain awake, not to go to bed)
   1. I want *to stay up* tonight and watch the late show.
   2. He *stays up* every night until after one o'clock, preparing his homework.

8. to stay in — to stay out: (*To stay in* is to remain at home, not to go out. *To stay out* means to be out of the house, not to be at home.)
   1. We *stay in* almost every night and watch television.
   2. He never *stays in* a single night. He goes out every night.
   3. Cal *stays out* every night until after midnight.

4.  I promised my mother that I would not *stay out* late tonight.

9.  to be into: (to have as an interest, particularly a study or style. Compare #6) (S) (very informal)
    1.  Kristin *is into* health foods; in fact, she has become a vegetarian.
    2.  George *was* really *into* astrology a lot last year. Is he still interested in the zodiac?
    3.  She's *into* purple this year; everything she owns is that color.

10. to take over: (to assume direction or control of) (S)
    1.  After the first of the month Angie will *take over* Mr. Fauntroy's duties.
    2.  Helen worked on the report for several days and then John *took over*.
    3.  When the publisher of that magazine retires, his daughter will *take it over*.

11. to show up: (to appear)
    1.  He promised to come on Tuesday but he never *showed up*.
    2.  Not one student *showed up* for the scheduled meeting.

*Boy, am I glad you showed up!*

12. to clean out — to clean off, etc.
    (Note: These forms are not idiomatic, but note how the addition of *out, off, up*, etc., changes slightly or makes the meaning of the verb more exact. Such usages are very common in English. See *to clean up*, Lesson 18, No. 10. Also compare: *to sweep out, to sweep off, to sweep up; to brush out, to brush off, to brush up, to wash out, to wash off, to wash up*, etc.) (S)
    1. I want you *to clean out* that closet (*to clean* that closet *out*) so that we can store these things in there.
    2. The waitress will *clean off* this table (*clean* this table *off*) in a moment.
    3. The maid will *clean up* the room before they arrive.
    4. *Sweep out* that room well.
    5. Mary is *sweeping off* the porch now.
    6. *Sweep up* those crumbs that are on the floor.
    7. There's an ant on your sleeve. Let me *brush it off*.
    8. After spraying my mouth with antiseptic, the dentist told me *to wash* it *out*.

# EXERCISES

A. Substitute an idiomatic expression for the word or words in italics. Make any necessary changes in the form of the verb in parentheses. Some substitutions may require other grammatical changes as well.

1. The riots were quickly *suppressed* by the police.

   (put_____ )
2. John *is very much interested in* sculpture as a hobby.

   (go _____ )
3. The loud noise of the rock music on the stereo is *making me nervous*.

   (get _____ )
4. How long have you *had an interest* in yoga?

   (be _____ )
5. We waited for hours but he never *appeared*.

   (show _____ )

6. The new cabinet officer will *assume* many of the duties of the president.

   (take _____ )

7. John *remains out of the house* every night until after midnight.

   (stay _____ )

8. We *did not go to bed* until twelve o'clock waiting for some word from John.

   (stay _____ )

9. They *remain at home* every night and read.

   (stay _____ )

10. Everything in the icebox *has the flavor of* garlic.

    (taste _____ )

**B.** Answer these questions, making use of the idiomatic expressions studied in this lesson.

1. Why did you *stay up* so late last night?

2. How late do you usually *stay up* at night?

3. Which member of your family generally *stays up* the latest?

4. Do you *stay in* every night during the school week or do you sometimes go out?

5. Do you *stay in* on Sunday nights or do you always go out?

6. Have you ever had to *make do* with old clothes because you couldn't afford new ones?

7. Why did you promise your mother that you would not *stay out* late last night?

8. Do you know anyone who *is into* gardening?

9. Who will *take over* the boss's duties when he goes on his vacation?

10. What is the difference in meaning between *to clean up* something and *to clean out* something?

11. What is the difference in meaning between these two sentences: "Please *clean out* this desk" amd "Please *clean off* this desk"?

12. Which is more correct to say: "Please *sweep* these crumbs" or "Please *sweep up* these crumbs"?

13. What sports do you *go in for?*

14. *Are* you more *into* fiction or nonfiction?

15. Why does this bread *taste of* onions?

16. Why does everything in the refrigerator *taste of* fish?

# LESSON 24

1. **to knock out:** (to render unconscious by a strong blow) (S)
   1. The prizefighter *knocked out* his opponent with one punch.
   2. The stone hit her on the head and *knocked* her *out* for a few minutes.
   3. The fight was won by a *knockout*.

2. **to carry out:** (to accomplish, execute, bring to a successful end) (S)
   1. They *carried out* their plan without difficulty.
   2. The men refused *to carry out* the captain's orders.
   3. It's easier to make plans than *to carry* them *out*.

3. **to run into—to run across:** (to meet or find unexpectedly; see also *to come across*, Lesson 22, No. 3)
   1. You will never guess whom I *ran into* on Grant Avenue yesterday.
   2. I *ran across* several interesting facts about Guatemala in that book.

4. **to set out:** (to begin, leave from a place or start toward a place)
   1. Janet *set out* to compete for the large scholarship grant; I hope she is successful.
   2. The soldiers obeyed their commander's orders and *set out* at dawn.
   3. Early the next morning Stanley *set out* on foot for Boston.

5. **to draw up:** (to prepare documents or legal papers) (S)
   1. Our lawyer will *draw up* the contract today.
   2. This agreement was not *drawn up* correctly, we'll have to do it again.
   3. If you want to make a will, you will have to have a lawyer *draw* one *up* for you.

6. to drop in or drop in on: (to call on or to visit unexpectedly)
   1. If you are ever in our neighborhood, be sure *to drop in on* us.
   2. Some old friends *dropped in on* us last night.
   3. *Drop in* tonight after work, if you can.

7. to drop out: (to leave, withdraw, cease attending)
   1. Many students have *dropped out* of school because of the economic recession.
   2. Two more teams have *dropped out* of the league.

8. to believe in: (to accept as true, have faith in the existence of)
   1. I really think that she *believes in* ghosts.
   2. Do you *believe in* God?

9. to cheer up: (to make happier, inspire) (S)
   1. We all tried *to cheer* her *up*, but she continued to feel sad.
   2. I have some good news which I am sure will *cheer* Kate *up*.
   3. The nurse tried *to cheer up* the little boy when he started to cry.

10. to make sense: (to be sensible, reasonable)
    1. Your socialistic plea to divide all the wealth does not *make* any *sense* to a capitalist.
    2. To send troops abroad when we need them here simply does not *make sense*.

*I'm worried — my parents are starting to make sense to me.*

11. to blow down—to blow off—to blow away, etc. (S) (Note: These forms are not idiomatic, but, like those studied in the last lesson, Lesson 23, No. 12, they are important, since they show how the particles *down, off, away,* etc., are often added to a verb to change the meaning slightly or to make the meaning more exact or more emphatic.) (S)
   1. The wind *blew down* the fence (*blew* the fence *down*).
   2. The roof of the house was *blown off* during the storm.
   3. I'm afraid the wind may *blow* the tent *away*.

12. to break down—to break through—to break away, etc. (S) (See note above on *to blow down, to blow off,* etc.)
   1. They *broke down* the door (*broke* the door *down*) and entered the room.
   2. Our troops finally *broke through* enemy lines.
   3. After a brief struggle, he *broke away* from the police.

# EXERCISES

A. Find and underline the expression corresponding to the italicized idiom above.

   1. If someone has been *knocked out*, he has been
      (a) kept out of the house.
      (b) visited.
      (c) made unconscious.

   2. If something doesn't *make sense*, it is not
      (a) funny.
      (b) expensive.
      (c) logical.

   3. To *cheer* someone *up* is to
      (a) criticize her.
      (b) make her feel happier.
      (c) lift her up.

   4. If someone *drops out*, he
      (a) begins.
      (b) is often absent.
      (c) leaves permanently.

   5. If someone *drops in on* me, she
      (a) visits me.
      (b) drops me a line.
      (c) gives me a call.

6. To *draw up* a contract is to
    (a) sign a contract.
    (b) prepare a contract.
    (c) look over a contract.

7. To *run across* someone is to
    (a) run over him.
    (b) run up to him.
    (c) meet him unexpectedly.

8. If I *set out* early, I
    (a) arrive early.
    (b) wake up early.
    (c) leave early.

9. If orders are *carried out*, they are
    (a) criticized.
    (b) not understood.
    (c) executed.

B. Answer these questions, making use of idiomatic expressions.

1. What time did Ed *set out* this morning to avoid heavy traffic?

2. Who did you *run into* on Fifth Avenue recently?

3. What is the difference between *to run into a person* and *to run over a person?*

4. What do we mean when we say that "Missy *ran into* a tree"?

5. What does *to run out* of something mean?

6. What old friends *dropped in on* you not so long ago?

7. Do you like to have friends *drop in on* you or do you prefer that they tell you in advance that they are coming?

8. Have any students *dropped out* of your English class this semester?

9. Why did that student *drop out* of school?

10. Is it easy or difficult *to knock out* a person?

11. Have you ever been *knocked out?*

12. Does a boxer win a fight by scoring a *knockout?* How?

13. What is the difference in meaning between, "His hat *blew off*" and "His hat *blew away*"?

14. What is the difference between *to break up something* and *to break down something?*

15. What is the difference in meaning between, "He *got out* of jail" and "He *broke out* of jail"?

# LESSON 25

1. **to burst out crying—to burst out laughing:** (to begin suddenly to laugh or to cry)
   1. John was quietly reading the joke book when he suddenly *burst out laughing.*
   2. Every time that she thought about her mother's death she *burst out crying* (also, *burst into tears*).

2. **to get away:** (to leave, escape)
   1. We always try *to get away* from the noise and heat of the city for a month or two each summer.
   2. My parents don't know yet when we can *get away* this summer.
   3. No one knows how the suspect managed *to get away* from the police.

3. **to get away with:** (to do something forbidden or illegal and to escape without punishment)
   1. I don't know how he *gets away with* it, but he comes late to the lesson almost every day.
   2. You can't be rude to everyone and expect *to get away with* it forever.

4. **to keep up:** (to maintain or continue the same speed or level) (S)
   1. If we can *keep up* this speed, we should arrive there in about two hours.
   2. The government wants *to keep* farm prices *up* at their present levels.
   3. That student has been getting all As. I hope he can *keep* it *up.*

5. **to make up:** (a. to compensate for some loss or absence. (S) b. to become reconciled after a quarrel. c. to invent or to fabricate. (S) d. cosmetics.)
   a. 1. If you miss a lesson, we can *make* it *up* later.

    **2.** Those unexcused absences must be *made up.*

    **3.** John was absent from the examination and has to take *a make-up* exam tomorrow.

**b.**  **1.** After the quarrel the two young lovers kissed and *made up.*

    **2.** Why don't you two children *make up* and forget all about your argument?

**c.**  **1.** That story John told wasn't true; he *made* it all *up.*

    **2.** She *made up* a long story about being out of town at the time, but no one believed her.

**d.**  **1.** Her *makeup* kit included four shades of eye shadow.

    **2.** Helen uses a lot of *makeup,* especially mascara.

**6.** to stand out: (to be prominent, outstanding)

    **1.** Her bright red hair made her *stand out* from the others.

    **2.** He is a tall, distinguished looking man who *stands out* in any crowd.

**7.** to let on: (to reveal what you know)

    **1.** Don't *let on* to Doris that we are going to the movies tonight. We don't want her to know.

    **2.** He asked me not *to let on* to anyone that we were planning the birthday party; it's a surprise.

*Don't let on that you see it.*

Jerry Van Amerongen

8. **to serve (one) right:** (to receive one's just punishment)
   1. It *served* him *right* to lose that job, because he neglected it.
   2. It *serves* you *right* to have lost your purse. You were always too careless about leaving it around.

9. **to go wrong:** (to fail, turn out badly)
   1. Something *went wrong* with the engine, and we had to have the car towed to the garage.
   2. I am sure that something has *gone wrong;* otherwise our guests would have arrived long ago.

10. **to meet (someone) halfway:** (to compromise)
    1. Our suppliers are ready *to meet* us *halfway* in the matter of price. They wanted us to pay $20, we wanted to pay $10, so we agreed on a price of $15.
    2. In an effort to end the strike, the owners agreed *to meet the* strikers *halfway.*

11. **to check up—to check on—to check up on:** (to check, examine, inspect)
    1. They are *checking on* that information right now to see if it's accurate.
    2. That employer has hired a detective *to check up on* all the employee's past activities for security.
    3. My doctor wants me to have a thorough *checkup.* She calls this preventive medicine.

12. **to stick up—to stick out:** (to protrude) (S)
    1. Your hair is *sticking up* in the back.
    2. I could see one end of the letter *sticking out* of John's pocket.
    3. The doctor told me *to stick out* my tongue, so I *stuck it out.*

# EXERCISES

A. Find and underline the expression given in parentheses that corresponds to the italicized idiom.

1. If, after a quarrel, two friends *make up*, this means that they
   (never speak to each other again, hate each other, become reconciled, come to blows).

2. If I say that Nell *made up* that story, I mean that she (told it well, invented it, repeated it several times).

3. To use *makeup* is to
   (go to extremes, tell lies, use cosmetics.)

4. If something *sticks out*, it
   (protrudes, is sticky, shines, aches).

5. *To get away with* something is to
   (enjoy it, do it repeatedly, do it and escape without punishment).

6. If someone *bursts out laughing*, he
   (laughs constantly, hurts himself, begins to laugh suddenly).

7. If I say that something *served* you *right*, I mean that you
   (had a good time, deserved it, received good service).

8. *To meet* someone *halfway* is to
   (argue with him, run into him, run over him, compromise with him).

9. *To stand out is* to
   (be prominent or outstanding, wait outside, stand in line).

10. *To let on* is to
    (wait, give permission, reveal, accept).

**B.** Answer these questions, making use of the idiomatic expressions studied in this lesson.

1. Why do you say that Chan, who never does her homework, will not *get away with* it for very long?

2. How does that file clerk manage *to get away with* coming late to the office every morning?

3. Why did it *serve* William *right* to lose his job?

4. Why did it *serve* Senator Ball *right* to be defeated in the election?

5. Have you ever *made up* with someone after an argument?

6. Do the women in your family use much *makeup?*

7. Why do actors and actresses have to use so much *makeup?*

8. Why did the thief *make up* that story about finding the money in the street?

9. Why did Tom's girl friend ask him not *to let on* to her sister that she was going to the dance?

10. Why did Mrs. Jones suddenly *burst out crying?*

11. Why did everyone in your English class suddenly *burst out laughing* when John got to class very late?

12. Why does that actor *stand out* in any group or crowd?

13. Why did the doctor tell you *to stick out* your tongue?

14. Whose pencil is that which is *sticking out* of Brenda's pocket?

# LESSON 26

1. to come about: (to happen result)
   1. How did the accident *come about*? I don't know.
   2. The flood *came about* as a result of the heavy spring rains.

2. to build up: (to increase, make stronger) (S)
   1. He needs to exercise *to build up* his strength.
   2. They *built up* their savings so that they could buy a new house.
   3. Attendance at that new play is so low that the producers are trying *to build* it *up* by advertising heavily.

3. to bring about: (to cause to happen) (S)
   1. The accident was *brought about* by John's carelessness.
   2. The heavy spring rains *brought about* the flood.
   3. What *brought about* Jill and Harry's divorce?

4. to die down: (to decrease, lessen in intensity)
   1. After the excitement of opening the gifts ended, the party *died down*.
   2. The room seemed warm enough so we let the fire *die down*. Now only embers are left.

5. to fade away: (to diminish gradually in the distance, referring to sound)
   1. The sound of the horn on the boat slowly *faded away* as it sailed out to sea.
   2. The parade passed and the music of the band gradually *faded away*.

6. to die out: (to disappear gradually but completely)
   1. The custom of wearing vests seems *to be dying out*.
   2. That style of dancing *died out* years ago.

7. to make out: (a. to decipher, to understand) (S) (b. to prepare something, such as a will, a check, etc.) (S)
   a. 1. The letter was so badly written that I could not *make out* what she was trying to say.
      2. No one could *make out* what he was talking about. It was very confusing.
      3. Can you tell me what the student has written here? I can't *make it out*.
   b. 1. The clerk *made out* a receipt and gave it to me.
      2. Harold, will you *make out* a check to pay the telephone bill; *make it out* to the phone company.

8. to live up to: (to reach or maintain a certain standard)
   1. It surprised me, but that car salesman *lived up to* all the promises he made.
   2. It was clear that that lazy student would never *live up to* his family's expectations.

9. to stand up for: (to insist on; also to defend, to support)
   1. If you don't *stand up for* your rights, no one else will do it for you.
   2. All through the faculty meeting Frank *stood up for* his friend who was being criticized so severely.

10. to stick to: (to adhere to, persevere, be constant)
    1. Although I moistened it, the flap doesn't *stick to* the envelope.
    2. He has had five different jobs in the last year because he never *sticks to* anything very long.
    3. If you *stick to* it long enough you can find the answer to that problem.

11. to stick (someone): (to cheat someone)
    1. Be careful dealing with him. He'll *stick you* at the first opportunity.
    2. They certainly *stuck me* when I bought this car. I have had trouble with it constantly.

12. to get stuck: (to be cheated, to become cheated — also to be burdened with)
    1. If you paid more than three hundred dollars for that old car, you *got stuck*.
    2. I certainly *got stuck* when I bought this raincoat; every time I go out in the rain, it shrinks some more.
    3. I *got stuck* with the task of providing entertainment at our annual office party.

# EXERCISES

**A.** Find and underline the expression corresponding to the italicized idiom above.

1. *To bring about* something is to
    (a) hear about it.
    (b) talk about it.
    (c) cause it to happen.

2. If something *dies out*, it
    (a) disappears completely.
    (b) begins.
    (c) grows in strength.

3. If a sound *fades away*, it
    (a) increases in intensity.
    (b) is musical.
    (c) diminishes gradually in the distance.

4. If I *build up* my strength, I
    (a) undermine it.
    (b) increase it.
    (c) underestimate it.

5. If, in buying something, I *get stuck*, I
    (a) get a good bargain.
    (b) can't resist it.
    (c) am cheated.

6. If I can't *make* something *out*, I can't
    (a) enjoy it.
    (b) do it.
    (c) understand it.

7. *To come about* is to
    (a) happen.
    (b) leave early.
    (c) arrive on time.

8. If turmoil begins to *die down*, it
    (a) diminishes in intensity.
    (b) increases in intensity.
    (c) moves to the basement.

9. If William never *sticks to* anything, he never
    (a) arrives on time.
    (b) stays at home.
    (c) perseveres or continues for a sufficient period of time.

10. He *stood up for* his friend means that he
    (a) gave his friend his seat.
    (b) defended him.
    (c) went out with him.

**B.** Answer these questions, making use of the idiomatic expressions studied in this lesson.

1. What is the difference between *building something* and *building something up?*

2. Does *come about* mean the same as *come across?* What is the difference?

3. Why were you unable *to make out* what those two men were talking about?

4. Why were you unable *to make out* what Mary had written in that note which she sent you?

5. What happens at the bank if a check is not *made out* correctly?

6. How did that accident which happened on the corner *come about?*

7. What *brought about* Jane's illness?

8. What finally *brought about* the end of the Vietnam War?

9. Why did Pedro *get stuck* when he bought those shoes?

10. Why did Mr. Smith *get stuck* when he bought that automobile?

11. Why does Nelson never seem *to stick to* any job for very long? Is he restless or does he get fired?

12. Why does the custom of wearing vests seem *to be dying out?*

13. Why do certain styles in men's and women's clothes *die out* more quickly than others?

14. Why did the sound of that music gradually *fade away?*

15. What is the difference between *to die down* and *to die out?*

# LESSON 27

1. **to take on:** (to employ, hire) (S)
   1. They are *taking on* a lot of new workers at that plant.
   2. We will have *to take on* someone to do Felix's work while he's away.
   3. If you like that new job applicant, let's *take* her *on*.

2. **to take down:** (to remove; also, to write what is said) (S)
   1. I want *to take down* the pictures and clean them.
   2. I'm going *to take down* those curtains and put up new ones.
   3. Her secretary *took down* everything we said.
   4. That stenographer *took down* the president's entire speech in shorthand.
   5. That concert notice is out of date. *Take* it *down*.

3. **to fall off:** (to fall from something; also, to decrease in volume)
   1. Henry *fell off* his bicycle and hurt his knee.
   2. The picture *fell off* the wall and broke.
   3. Our sales have been *falling off* seriously during the past six months.
   4. Business conditions are bad at present and our sales representative's commissions have *fallen off*.

4. **to fall through:** (to fail to materialize, collapse)
   1. Our plans for a big picnic *fell through* when it rained.
   2. We wanted to go to Europe this summer but our plans *fell through* when we failed to save enough money.

5. **to fall behind:** (to lag, fail to keep up)
   1. Eve *fell behind* in her studies and finally had to leave school.
   2. If you *fall behind* in your payments, the finance company may take your car back.

6. **to give in:** (to surrender)
   1. Completely surrounded by our troops, the enemy finally *gave in*.
   2. They *gave in* to the strikers' demands and agreed to a 36-hour work week.

7. **to give off:** (to release, produce)
   1. When you boil water it *gives off* steam.
   2. The flowers *gave off* a strange odor.

8. **to give out:** (a. to distribute (S); b. to become exhausted, terminate)
   a. 1. An usher stood at the door *giving out* programs.

2. They *gave out* a sample of the perfume to each customer who came to the counter.

**b.** 1. When their ammunition *gave out,* the troops had to surrender.

2. I plan to stay there until my money *gives out*.

3. The chair *gave out* under the extra weight and collapsed.

9. **to have it in for:** (to dislike, hold a grudge, wait for an opportunity for revenge)

1. Martina expects to lose her job because the boss has *had it in for* her for a long time.

2. The teacher has *had it in for* Al ever since the time that he insulted her in front of the class.

10. **to have it out with:** (to quarrel with, confront, bring into the open)

1. I have suspected him of lying for a long time, and today we are going *to have it out with* him.

2. Instead of waiting for the arrival of the police, it is better *to have it out with* the thief right away.

11. **to hold off:** (to delay)

1. If the rain *holds off* for a few days more, they can finish the planting.

2. Their attorney has promised *to hold off* legal action for another week.

12. **to hold out:** (a. to continue in supply, prove to be sufficient; b. to resist)

**a.** 1. If our supplies *hold out,* we will camp here for another week.

2. I will stay in Mexico as long as my money *holds out*.

**b.** Our troops cannot *hold out* much longer against the superior forces of the enemy.

13. **to hold over:** (to continue something, postpone) (S)

1. They are going *to hold* that movie *over* for another week; it's very successful.

2. Let's *hold over* discussion of this problem until our next meeting.

14. **to turn over:** (a. to invert, place upside down; b. to transfer to another) (S)

**a.** 1. The car *turned over* twice before falling into the river.

2. If you *turn over* a turtle on its back, it becomes helpless.

3. That record is finished. *Turn* it *over* to play the other side.
b. 1. Mr. Collins will *turn over* his work to Ms. Giles when he goes away.
2. He has decided *to turn over* his business to his son.
3. The victim *turned* the pieces of the exploded bomb *over* to the police.

# EXERCISES

A. Substitute an idiomatic expression for the word or words in italics. Make any necessary changes in the form of the verb in parentheses. Some substitutions may require other grammatical changes as well.

1. A secretary *wrote* everything the prisoner said.

   (take _____ )

2. Our sales have been *decreasing* recently.

   (fall _____ )

3. They are *hiring* many new workers at that factory.

   (take _____ )

4. The material, when wet, *produces* a strong smell.

   (give _____ )

5. She has *waited for revenge on* him for a long time.

   (have it _____ )

6. He will *transfer* all his property to his wife.

   (turn _____ )

7. The car struck a tree and *inverted* three times.

   (turn _____ )

8. They are going *to extend the showing of* that movie for another week.

   (hold _____ )

9. If my money *is sufficient*, I will stay another month.

   (hold _____ )

10. They are beginning *to lag* in their payments.

   (fall _____ )

11. Our plans for a big holiday dance *collapsed*.

(fall _____ )

12. He argued so long that I finally *surrendered* to him.

(give _____ )

**B.** Answer these questions, making use of the idiomatic expressions studied in this lesson.

1. Why did the plans for a school dance *fall through?*

2. Why did Irma's plans to travel abroad this summer *fall through?*

3. What happens if someone *falls behind* in his payments on the mortgage on his home?

4. What will happen to you if you *fall behind* in your school work?

5. Why did our troops finally *give in* to the enemy?

6. Why did the owners eventually have *to give in* to the strikers' demands?

7. Why has the movie at your local drive-in been *held over* for another week?

8. Why has the teacher *had it in for* Mary for a long time?

9. What accounts for the fact that sales have been *falling off* recently?

10. Did that man *fall off* the roof or was he pushed by someone?

11. Why did a secretary *take down* everything that the witness told the police captain?

12. Why are they *taking on* so many new workers at that plant?

13. Why is Mr. Vale *turning over* his business to his daughter?

14. Which car *turned over* twice in the accident, yours or the other person's?

15. Why does a turtle become helpless if you *turn it over* on its back?

# LESSON 28

1. **to let up:** (to slacken, lessen in intensity)
   1. If the rain *lets up* a little, they may begin the parade.
   2. It has snowed for three days without *letting up.*

2. **to lay off:** (to dismiss temporarily, generally because of lack of work) (S)
   1. During this season of the year they often *lay off* many workers at that plant.
   2. If business continues to be slow, we may have *to lay off* one or two people.
   3. Was Pete fired or *laid off?*
   4. Bill hasn't lost his job. His firm *laid* him *off* for two weeks.

3. **to bring out:** (to produce, to present) (S)
   1. They try *to bring out* one new book each month.
   2. Most of the automobile companies *bring out* new models each year.
   3. The clerk *brought out* several different types of gloves for us to examine.
   4. We wanted to see some old family pictures so Jennie *brought* them *out* and showed them to us.

4. **to bring back—to take back:** (to return) (S)
   1. If you don't like the dress you bought, you can always *bring* it *back* with the sales receipt.
   2. You can borrow my car if you promise *to bring* it *back* tomorrow.
   3. Have you *brought back* my screwdriver yet?
   4. If I were you, I'd *take* those gloves *back.* They are much too small.
   5. I *took* the book *back* to the library yesterday.

5. **to wait up for:** (to wait until very late without going to bed at the usual time)
   1. Don't *wait up for* me tonight. I may be very late.
   2. We *waited up for* him until two o'clock and then finally went to bed.

6. **to let (someone or something) alone:** (to permit to be alone, avoid, stay away from)
   1. *Let* him *alone* for a while and he may go to sleep.
   2. The plant will grow much better if you *let it alone.*
   3. After the dog had bitten him once or twice, Peter *let* it *alone.*

7. **let alone:** (not to mention, to say nothing of, certainly not) (Used after negative clauses)
    1. I'm so sick today that I couldn't walk as far as the kitchen *let alone* go to the zoo with you.
    2. He doesn't even speak his own language well, *let alone* French.

8. **to break off:** (to terminate, put an end to; see also Lesson 19, No. 1) (S)
    1. We may *break off* relations with that country.
    2. Diplomatic relations were *broken off* between the two countries several years before the war began.
    3. Elsa and Bob were engaged, but they have *broken* it *off*.

9. **to wear off:** (to disappear gradually)
    1. My headache isn't serious. It will *wear off* after an hour or so.
    2. The effect of the painkilling drug did not *wear off* for several hours.

10. **to wear down—to wear away—to wear through:** (to reduce gradually through the process of wear; see *to wear out*, Lesson 8, No.7) (S)
    1. The heels of your shoes are *worn down* on one side.
    2. The constant washing of the sea against the rocks gradually *wears* them *away*.
    3. The seat of his pants was *worn through*.
    4. He had *worn through* his coat at the elbows.
    5. Helga threw away that dress because she had *worn* it *out*.

11. **on the whole;** (in general in most ways)
    1. He is, *on the whole*, a good student.
    2. *On the whole*, I agree with you.
    3. *On the whole*, business has been good this year.

12. **to read over:** (to glance over—to run over) (S)
    Note: The particle *over*, when added to verbs, gives the meaning of examining something from beginning to end but in a rather rapid or superficial manner.
    1. The teacher said that she didn't have time to correct my composition, but she did *read* it *over*.
    2. He *glanced over* my report and said that it seemed to be all right.
    3. Let's *run over* this new list of prices once more.

*On the whole, Dad, don't you think it would be easier to support me for the rest of my life?*

# EXERCISES

**A.** Find and underline the expression given in parentheses that corresponds to the italicized word or words.

1. *To break off* relations with another country is to (desire relations with them, terminate relations, increase trade with them).

2. If I *take* something *back,* I (return it, borrow it, lend it).

3. If someone has been *dismissed temporarily from his job* because of lack of work, he has been (fired, hired, laid off).

4. *To wait up for* is to (wait standing up, wait for a short time, wait until late without going to bed.)

5. If the rain *lets up,* it (slackens, rains harder, rains constantly.)

6. If the seat of someone's trousers is *worn through*, it (is shiny, is spotted, has a hole in it, has worn well).

7. If something *wears off,* it
(disappears gradually, breaks down, lasts a long time).

8. *On the whole* means
(entirely, occasionally, in general)

9. *To read over* something is to
(read it rather hurriedly, read it with great interest, read it again and again).

10. Which of these can *wear down:*
(your coat, your gloves, your heels)?

**B.** Answer these questions, making use of the idiomatic expressions studied in this lesson.

1. With what different countries has the United States *broken off* diplomatic relations at one time or another?

2. Was that efficient worker fired from his job or *laid off?*

3. Why do some factories or industries *lay off* workers during certain periods of the year?

4. What is the difference in meaning between *to take on someone* and *to lay off someone?*

5. Why do most of the automobile manufacturers try *to bring out* new models of their cars each year?

6. What is the difference between *to wait for someone* and *to wait up for someone?*

7. Why did Sarah tell her mother not *to wait up for* her when she went out last night?

8. For how many days has it rained without *letting up?*

9. What is meant by saying that Hubert can't speak Spanish well, *let alone* French?

10. How long does it take for the effects of a drug such as aspirin *to wear off?*

11. What do you do when the heels of your shoes become *worn down?*

12. What is the difference between *to wear down* and *to wear away?*

13. What do we mean when we say that something has *worn through?*

14. If the soles of your shoes are *worn through,* what must you do?

15. Can you explain the difference between *to read* something and *to read over* something?

16. What is the difference in meaning between *to look at something* and *to look over something?*

# LESSON 29

1. **to work out:** (to develop, devise, turn out) (S)
    1. Don't worry. Everything will *work out* all right.
    2. We must *work out* some plan to increase our sales.
    3. I can't give you a promotion this year, but I believe I can *work* it *out* next July.

2. **to back up:** (to put a car in reverse, drive or go backwards) (S)
    1. Main Street was blocked with traffic, so I *backed up* and drove down one of the side streets.
    2. *Back up* a few feet more and then you can get out.
    3. If you want to get your car in that tight space, you'll have *to back* it *up* some more.

3. **to back out:** (to withdraw, fail to fulfill a promise or obigation)
    1. At the last minute John *backed out* and refused to go with us.
    2. We were all ready to sign the agreements when Ms. Bailey *backed out*.

4. **to be set (to do something)** (to be ready, prepared to do something)
    1. We *were all set* to leave when it started to rain.
    2. We *were all set* to sign the agreement when Mrs. Garfunkle backed out.

5. **to sit in:** (to participate as a member, also *to sit in on*)
    1. Mason, we're having a board meeting and we'd like you to *sit in*.
    2. I've been *sitting in on* the committee's hearings, and I think they should be open to the public.

*Did you have your heart set on the fresh chicken, sir?*

6. to have (one's) heart set on: (to desire greatly)
    1. She *has* her *heart set on* taking a trip abroad. She's been dreaming about it for months.
    2. For years he has *had* his *heart set on* buying that beach house. He really wants it.

7. to buy up: (to buy the complete stock of) (S)
    1. The government plans *to buy up* all surplus grain in order to stabilize the price.
    2. Russia is trying *to buy up* all the available tin.
    3. If you have any real silver quarters, the dealers are *buying* them *up* at a premium.

8. to buy out: (to buy a business) (S)
    1. He can sell his interest in that business any time because Mr. Bame will gladly *buy* him *out*.
    2. He has been trying for some time *to buy out* his partner.

9. to sell out: (to sell completely, liquidate) (S)
    1. The day of the blackout, most stores *sold out* their entire stock of flashlights within a few hours.
    2. There was a sign on the ticket office saying: "All *Sold Out*."
    3. The sign in the shop window read: "Big Sale! Tremendous Savings! *Selling Out!*"

10. to catch on: (to understand, particularly to grasp the meaning of a humorous story)
    1. To me it was a very funny story, but when I told it nobody seemed *to catch on*.
    2. Did you *catch on* to what Jody said?
    3. Since she doesn't understand English well, she did not *catch on* to any of the jokes we told.

11. to be cut out for—to be cut out to be: (to be designed for, have talent for)
    1. John *is* certainly not *cut out to be* a lawyer.
    2. Why should I try to do that kind of work when I know very well that I *am* not *cut out for* it?

12. to throw out: (to dismiss, eject by force) (S)
    1. The case was *thrown out* of court because of insufficient evidence.
    2. When one of the customers got drunk, they immediately *threw* him *out* of the cafe.

13. to throw up: (to vomit) (S)
    1. Mac got sick and *threw up* everything he had eaten.
    2. When I get seasick, I *throw up* my food.
    3. The patient is unable to digest her food: she is *throwing it all up*

14. to clear up: (to become clear, to clarify) (S)
    1. The newspaper says that the weather is going *to clear up* tomorrow.
    2. As soon as Henry arrives, he will *clear up* this problem by explaining what we should do.
    3. That murder was a mystery for a long time, but a clever detective *cleared* it *up*.

# EXERCISES

A. Substitute, in place of the italicized word or words, the corresponding idiomatic expression partially indicated in parentheses.

   1. At the last minute John *withdrew from* the agreement.

      (back _____ )

   2. He put the car in reverse and *drove backwards*.

      (back _____ )

3. We have *to seek and develop* a new method.

   (work _____ )

4. Maryanne *participated in* the meeting as a non-voting member.

   (sit _____ )

5. He *desires greatly* to become a doctor.

   (have his heart _____ )

6. Nobody except Helen *understood* the joke.

   (catch _____ )

7. They *completely sold* their stock of shoes.

   (sell _____ )

8. They want *to purchase the entire supply of* that metal.

   (buy _____ )

9. He was *ejected by force from* the meeting.

   (throw _____ )

10. I *have no talent* for that kind of work.

    (cut out _____ )

B. Answer these questions, making use of the idiomatic expressions studied in this lesson.

   1. Why do students think that Miss Bacon *is* not *cut out to be* a teacher?

   2. Why is Tony not *cut out to be* a mechanic? What *is* she *cut out for*?

   3. Why was the gate-crasher *thrown out* of the theater?

   4. Why did they *throw* that noisy drunk *out* of the restaurant?

   5. Why does Albert *have* his *heart set on* being a doctor?

   6. Why does that artist *have* her *heart set on* going to Mexico this summer?

   7. Is there something *on* which you personally *have* your *heart set* at the present time?

   8. In driving an automobile, is it easier to drive forward or *to back up*?

   9. What do we mean when we say, "Kim *backed up* into a tree?"

10. Why did Jack's wife *back out of* her agreement to go camping with him?

11. What do you think of people who at the last moment *back out* of their promises or agreements?

12. Why would an owner wish *to sell out* his interest in a business?

13. What does an "All *Sold Out*" sign outside a theater ticket office mean?

14. If Mr. Jones wants *to buy out* his partner in that business, whose consent must he get?

15. What is the difference between *to buy something* and *to buy up something*?

16. What is the difference between *to buy up* and *to buy out*?

17. What is the difference between *to sit* and *to sit in on*?

# LESSON 30

1. to slow down: (to go more slowly) (S)
   1. There were signs at every curve in the road warning motorists *to slow down*.
   2. I told him several times *to slow down*, but he paid no attention.
   3. That racing car is so powerful that it is impossible to *slow* it *down* to a normal speed.

2. to dry up: (to dry completely) (S)
   1. Every summer the extreme heat in this valley *dries* the stream *up*.
   2. It rained very little and the streets soon *dried up*.

3. to dry out: (to become dry through a gradual loss of moisture) (S)
   1. If you don't cover the bread, it will soon *dry out*.
   2. We can't burn this wood. It is too green and not *dried out*.
   3. Martha hung up her towel in order to *dry* it *out*.

4. to be up to (something): (to be planning or plotting something, scheming)

   1.  What are those two boys *up to?* Some mischief, I'll bet.

   2.  Some people believe those men are spies, but no one knows what they are *up to.*

   3.  I thought you were *up to* no good when I saw you playing tricks on the cat.

**5.**  to beat around the bush: (to be indirect in approaching something)

   1.  Instead of *beating around the bush*, Melinda came straight to the point.

   2.  Our boss *beats around the bush* so much that no one knows exactly what he wants.

**6.**  to come to an end: (to terminate, cease)

   1.  The meeting finally *came to an end* at ten o'clock.

   2.  I thought that the movie would never *come to an end.*

**7.**  to put an end to: (to cause to end, to terminate in a definite manner)

   1.  You must *put an end to* that kind of malicious gossip.

   2.  It is up to the police *to put an end* to these robberies.

**8.**  to get even with: (to get revenge, retaliate)

   1.  Jerry once played a mean trick on John, and now John wants *to get even with* him.

   2.  I'll *get even with* you for breaking my sister's heart.

**9.**  to fool around: (to play and joke, spend time foolishly with little result)

   1.  Quit *fooling around* and get to work.

   2.  He is capable, but he *fools around* too much: he jokes with other workers or calls his friend on the telephone.

**10.**  to look out on: (to face, overlook)

   1.  Our apartment *looks out* on the river.

   2.  Their rear windows *look out on* a lovely garden.

**11.**  to stir up: (arouse, incite) (S)

   1.  He's always trying *to stir up* everyone with his arguments about politics.

   2.  They are trying *to stir up* trouble between the owners of the team and the players.

   3.  The boss is in a bad mood today so don't *stir* her *up* with any more customer complaints.

**12.**  to take in: (a. to visit  b. to decrease in size  c. to deceive) (S)

   a.  We decided *to take in* Toronto while we were traveling across Canada last summer. While we were there, we *took in* a movie at their largest theater.

  **b.** Lois lost weight and her waist got smaller, so she had to have her skirts and slacks *taken in*.

  **c.** Joseph *took* everyone *in* with his innocent manner; in fact, he was a liar and a cheat.

# EXERCISES

**A.** Find and underline the expression corresponding to the italicized idiom above.

**1.** If I *put an end to* something, I
  (a) delay it.
  (b) terminate it definitely.
  (b) slow it down.

**2.** If I *get even with* someone, I
  (a) borrow from him.
  (b) lend him money.
  (c) get revenge on him.

**3.** If someone *fools around* a great deal, he
  (a) wastes much time.
  (b) has a sense of humor.
  (c) telephones his friends.

**4.** If someone is *taken in*, she is
  (a) promoted.
  (b) invited to attend.
  (c) deceived.

**5.** If something *looks out on* the park, it
  (a) resembles the park.
  (b) faces the park.
  (c) is as large as the park.

**6.** When a driver *slows down*, she
  (a) stops.
  (b) goes more slowly.
  (c) gets nervous.

**7.** If bread *dries out*, it
  (a) tastes fresh.
  (b) loses its moisture.
  (c) has just come out of the oven.

**8.** If someone is *up to* something, he is
  (a) upstairs doing something.
  (b) in prison.
  (c) plotting something.

9. To *beat around the bush* is to
   (a) go hunting.
   (b) be direct in approaching something.
   (c) be indirect in approaching something.

10. When something *dries up,* it
    (a) becomes completely dry.
    (b) remains partly wet.
    (c) gets soaking wet.

---

Answer these questions, making use of the idiomatic expressions studied in this lesson.

1. What can be done in order to prevent bread from *drying out?*

2. Does bread become harder or softer when it *dries out?*

3. If the sun comes out, how long does it take the streets *to dry up* after a rainstorm?

4. Why do many mountain streams *dry up* during certain seasons of the year?

5. What are you *up to* now?

6. Why do you think that those boys are *up to* some trick or other?

7. Why did you think the meeting last night would never *come to an end?*

8. In what year did World War II finally *come to an end?*

9. Why are there so many signs along that road warning motorists *to slow down?*

10. If John had *slowed down* before reaching the corner, would the accident have happened?

11. What is the name of the park that that tall apartment house *looks out on?*

12. Why was that student so anxious *to get even with* his roommate?

13. How might a teacher *get even with* a student who insulted her?

14. Why did the teacher tell William to stop *fooling around* and to get to work?

15. Why did Henry *beat around the bush* so long instead of directly inviting Mary to the dance?

16. Have you ever had to have any of your clothes *taken in*?

17. Have you ever been *taken in* by someone you trusted but who later turned out to be untrustworthy?

# LESSON 31

1. to go through: (a. to endure, undergo, experience; b. go or be put into effect using *with*)
   a. 1. You will never know what she *went through* to educate her children.
      2. Soldiers *go through* a thorough physical training.
   b. 1. His application finally *went through*.
      2. Are they *going through with* their plans to build a new home?

2. to go without saying: (to be perfectly clear without the necessity of mentioning)
   1. It *goes without saying* that you shouldn't play with a loaded gun.
   2. That she will gain weight if she continues to eat so many pizzas *goes without saying*.

3. to put (someone) on: (to mislead) (S)
   1. Don't worry. I wouldn't ask you to do that. I'm just *putting* you *on*.
   2. You can't be serious! You must be *putting* me *on*!

4. to keep (one's) head: (to remain calm during some emergency)
   1. The astronauts *kept* their *heads* throughout all the excitement. They were always very self-controlled.
   2. Gloria *kept* her *head* and telephoned the fire department immediately; otherwise the whole house might have burned down.

5. to lose (one's) head: (to become very excited, lose one's self control)
   1. If that politician hadn't gotten angry and *lost* his *head*, he never would have slandered his opponent.

2. Seeing the other car coming toward him, at such speed, Mel *lost* his *head* and drove up over the curb into a tree.

6. to cut in: (to interrupt, enter sharply into the path of another)
   1. We were talking quietly when she *cut in* loudly and began to tell us about her trip.
   2. They were driving along slowly when another car *cut in* ahead of them.

7. to make room for: (to create space for, accommodate)
   1. Sit here with us. We can move over and *make room for* you on this sofa.
   2. Please join us. We can easily *make room for* one more at this table.

8. to stand up: (a. to withstand use or wear; b. to fail to appear, intentionally leave someone waiting at an appointment) (S)
   a. 1. The leather in these shoes will *stand up* much better than the leather in those you just tried on.
      2. Do you think your car will *stand up* well under such snowy conditions?
   b. 1. After waiting for two hours, Jim began to realize that Helen had *stood* him *up*.
      2. I didn't know whether he had forgotten about the appointment or whether he was *standing* me *up*.

*Make room for one more, Kitty.*

9. to get the better of: (to win or defeat, gain the advantage over a customer, etc.)
   1. He easily *got the better of* her in that argument.
   2. Be careful in dealing with him because he will try *to get the better of* you.

10. to break loose: (to become free or loose, escape)
    1. During the storm, the boat *broke loose* from the landing.
    2. He *broke loose* from the police and ran away.

11. to waste (one's) breath—to save one's breath: (to lose time talking in an ineffective effort to convince someone of something—to waste no words)
    1. Don't argue with Frank any longer. You are only *wasting* your *breath* trying to get him to agree with you.
    2. I tried to convince him that he was wrong, but I could see that I was only *wasting* my *breath*.
    3. *Save your breath!* Don't even mention your illness to your boss; she won't give you the afternoon off.

12. to cut short: (to make shorter, interrupt) (S)
    1. The meeting was *cut short* when the speaker got sick.
    2. The bad news from home *cut* our trip *short*.
    3. If you have anything more to say, please *cut* it *short* as your time is nearly up.

# EXERCISES

A. Find and underline the expression given in parentheses that corresponds to the italicized idiom.

1. If someone *loses* his *head*, he
   (becomes dizzy, becomes very excited, can't find something).

2. If something is *cut short*, it is
   (ended abruptly, attacked, made more lively).

3. If something *stands up well*, it
   (grows well, wears well, looks tall).

4. If someone *stands you up*, he
   (writes to you often, meets you on a corner, fails to meet you at an appointed place).

5. *To keep* one's *head* is to
   (remain calm, talk very little, get excited).

6. To *put* someone *on* is to
   (pretend, not mention, remain calm).

7. If something *goes without saying*, it is
   (on everybody's tongue, clear without mentioning it,
   confusing to everyone).

8. If something *breaks loose*, it
   (becomes free, gets lost, sinks).

9. *Save your breath* means
   (don't walk so fast, don't breathe so hard, don't lose
   time trying to convince someone of something).

10. *To cut in* ahead of someone is to
    (drive slowly, enter sharply into the path of another,
    apply the brakes quickly).

**B.** Answer these questions, making use of the idiomatic
expressions in this lesson.

1. How did that boat *break loose* from its mooring? Did
   someone cut the rope or did it break?

2. How did the dog *break loose* from its owner?

3. Why is it a *waste* of *breath* to argue with a person with
   a closed mind about politics?

4. Why was Mr. Smith's trip to Europe *cut short*?

5. Why was one of your classes *cut short*?

6. Have the shoes which you are wearing *stood up* well or
   have they been a disappointment?

7. Which will *stand up* better, a suit made of polyester or
   one made of wool?

8. Have you ever been *stood up* by anyone?

9. Why is it sometimes a rather humiliating experience *to
   be stood up*?

10. Why is it dangerous, while driving, *to cut in* ahead of
    another car?

11. What does it mean when you're dancing if someone
    taps on your shoulder and asks, "May I *cut in*?"

12. Why do people say that *it goes without saying* that Cindy
    is the most popular girl in the school?

13. Why does *it go without saying* that the United States
    today must play an important part in world affairs?

14. What did you do the last time you *put* someone *on*?

15. Are you the type of person who, in an emergency,
    *keeps her head* or *loses her head*?

# REVIEW

LESSONS 1–31

**A.** In the blank sentences at the right, give a ONE-WORD synonym for the italicized word or words. Follow the example in the first sentence.

1. Some friends *dropped in on* us last night. _____visited_____

2. The plane *took off* at exactly ten o'clock. _____

3. I *came across* an old friend on Fifth Avenue yesterday. _____

4. He is a man that everyone *looks up to*. _____

5. The troops easily *put down* the riot. _____

6. We waited until ten o'clock but she never *showed up*. _____

7. They *set out* at dawn on their camping trip. _____

8. The lawyer will *draw up* the contract tomorrow. _____

9. In this code each number *stands for* a letter of the alphabet. _____

10. Many students have *dropped out of* our class. _____

11. No one knows how she managed to *get away* from the police. _____

12. I am sure that Jim *made up* that story. _____

13. How did such a strange thing *come about*? _____

14. The sounds of their voices gradually *died away*. _____

15. Zelda *is into* transcendental meditation as a means of relaxation. _____

16. I can't *make out* what she means in this telegram. _____

17. You have *made out* this check incorrectly. _____

18. Did you *take in* the Rodin exhibit at the National Gallery last month? _____

19. They are *taking on* more workers at that factory. _____

20. Last month they had to *lay off* several hundred workers. _____

21. Our sales have *fallen off* recently. _____

22. An usher stood at the door *giving out* programs. _____

23. The car *turned over* twice before landing in the lake. _____

24. He will *turn over* all his property to his children. _____

25. As soon as the rain *lets up*, we will leave. _____

26. The effects of the drug will *wear off* in a few hours. _____

27. You must *put an end* to such foolishness. _____

28. Our apartment *looks out on* the Columbia University campus. _____

29. They are trying to *stir up* trouble among the smaller nations. _____

30. We were all *taken in* by his smooth manner of talking. _____

B. Substitute, in place of the italicized word or words, an idiomatic expression with *to get*. (Examples: *get on, get off, get up, get along, get along with, get back, get over, get to, get sick, get in touch with, get used to, get rid of, get through, get lost, get on one's nerves, get away, get away with, get even with*)

   1. You can *communicate with* him at his home tonight.

   2. We will never *arrive in* Boston at this speed.

   3. Mr. and Mrs. White do not *live together harmoniously*.

4. Sooner or later I will *get revenge on* her.
5. That music is beginning *to make me nervous.*
6. He will never *recover from* the death of his son.
7. When do you expect *to return* from Cuba?
8. How are you *doing* in your English lessons?
9. At what corner do you *board* the bus every morning?
10. At what stop do you *leave* the bus every morning?
11. At what time do you *arise* each morning?
12. When I eat fish I always *become ill.*
13. We have mice in our apartment and we can't seem *to lose* or *exterminate* them.
14. What time each night do you *finish* working?

C. Give sentences illustrating the difference between the following pairs of idiomatic expressions.

| | |
|---|---|
| to get on—to get off | to wait for—to wait up for |
| to call on—to call off | to eat in—to eat out |
| to put on—to put off | to take off—to take on |
| to call up—to call down | to break up—to break down |
| to take out—to take in | to give in—to give out |
| to put up—to put down | to hold on—to hold off |
| to keep on—to keep off | to turn off—to turn on |
| to look up to—to look down on | to take up—to take down |

D. Select the appropriate rejoinder, question, or continuation of the statement. Note the italicized idiom in deciding on your answer.

1. Zan and Rich *pulled off* one of the best jokes I've ever witnessed.
   a. Yes, they always fail, don't they?
   b. How did they do it?
   c. Did it hurt when it came off?

2. *According to* my watch, we're a few minutes early.
   a. Well I'm glad we're here on time.
   b. How well do you play your accordion?
   c. How late are we?

3. I want you to wait here *in case* I need you tonight.
   a. In which case do you want me to wait?
   b. All right, I'll keep myself available.
   c. Is it time to leave yet?

4. Did you *get carried away* when you described the beauty of their garden?
   a. No, I wouldn't let them lift me.
   b. Yes, I left because I hated it.
   c. Yes, I even started to cry.

5. Will you *sit in on* that meeting for me, please. I have to leave early.
   a. I'd be happy to attend and take notes.
   b. I've been standing up all day.
   c. I've been sitting down all day.

6. I think I'll *take pity on* those poor people who are begging for money.
   a. I see them too.
   b. I feel sorry for them too.
   c. I can't stand them either.

7. Maureen says that we're scheduled *to take off* at 6:05.
   a. That's a lot of people to hire.
   b. I'm cold, so I think I'll leave my sweater on.
   c. We'd better leave for the airport now.

8. That factory *gives off* an unbelievable odor when it's working at full capacity.
   a. What can we do to combat it?
   b. When did you surrender?
   c. I'm glad they finally conceded.

9. *Cut it out!* You can't do that here.
   a. I didn't realize that I was interrupting you.
   b. May I have some different scissors?
   c. I didn't realize that I was bothering you. I'll stop.

# LESSON 32

1. **to have two strikes against (one):** (to be in a disadvantageous position or in danger)
   1. I wanted to play the role of a young boy in that play, but I *had two strikes against* me—my age and my height; I was too old and too tall for the part.
   2. Anyone who has two unexcused absences from this office *has two strikes against him.*

2. **to step down:** (to retire or leave a top position)
   1. Next May our company's president will *step down,* and we will have to elect a new one at the next stockholders' meeting.
   2. In a couple of years that high school principal will *step down,* and her job will be taken by the vice-principal.

3. **to be a steal:** (to be a bargain)
   1. On Washington's Birthday we bought a $395 color television set for $89. That's *a steal.*
   2. What *a steal* that Wedgwood jar that we bought at a church fair was.

4. **to play up to:** (to flatter to gain or keep good favor with)
   1. Because that securities dealer *plays up to* wealthy old ladies so well, he makes a fortune on commissions.
   2. Doreen has been *playing up to* the boss in the hopes that she will get a promotion.

5. **more or less:** (nearly, approximately, somewhat)
   1. Your bedroom is *more or less* the same size as mine.
   2. I believe that it will cost *more or less* $300 to get the TV set repaired.
   3. Do you believe in ghosts? Yes, I do, *more or less.*

6. **to screw up:** (to mix up or spoil something) (S)
   1. That ignorant repairman certainly *screwed up* my television set.
   2. He's been *screwing* this *up* long enough. It's time we get a more competent leader.
   3. What a *screw-up* Bert is! He never gets anything right.

7. **to be rained out:** (said of a sports event or any other outdoor activity that has to be postponed or called off on account of rain)
   1. That baseball game that we had planned to watch on TV *was rained out.* They showed an old movie instead.
   2. We didn't know that that outdoor tennis match *had been rained out* and so we had to drive back home without seeing it.

8. to go off the deep end: (to do something hastily, rashly, or dangerously)
    1. Just because you argued with your supervisor, you didn't have *to go off the deep end* and resign, did you?
    2. If reporters ask you for information, give them as much as they are entitled to, but don't *go off the deep end.*

9. to lose (one's) touch: (to fail at what one used to do well, to cease to interest others)
    1. Milton used to sell more cars than any other of our salesmen did, but lately he has been *losing* his *touch* and is way behind the other men in sales.
    2. That movie star used to have lots of fans, but in recent years she has *lost* her *touch.*

10. to have (something) going for (one): (to be successful in some undertaking, attribute, or field of interest)
    1. With her brains and beauty Alma certainly *has* every- thing *going for* her.
    2. Although she is only eighteen, that young dress designer *has* something *going for* her, as is shown by the heavy demand for her dresses.
    3. The movie star may not be able to act, but he does *have* good looks *going for* him.

11. on the double!: (Hurry! quickly)
    1. Here it is nine o'clock and you two television watchers haven't done the dishes yet. *On the double!*
    2. I want that report from your office *on the double!*

12. on hand: (available, nearby)
    1. I always keep an extra $10 bill *on hand* in case of an emergency.
    2. Blake likes to have his lawyer *on hand* for all of his serious negotiations.

A. Find and underline the expression corresponding to the italicized idiom above.

**EXERCISES**

1. If a mechanic *screws up* your car, he
    (a) publicizes it.
    (b) ruins it.
    (c) improves it.

2. When a person *goes off the deep end,* she
    (a) acts rashly.
    (b) dives into the deeper water.
    (c) gets lost.

3. When that opera singer *plays up to* the conductor, she
    (a) plays a musical instrument for him.
    (b) takes his place.
    (c) flatters and seeks to interest him.

4. When someone *has* something *going for* himself, he
    (a) is successful in some enterprise or undertaking.
    (b) has his watch ticking.
    (c) is being arrested.

5. If something *is a steal,* it is
    (a) a stolen article.
    (b) an act of theft.
    (c) a bargain.

6. When a person *has two strikes against* her, she is
    (a) badly injured.
    (b) on strike.
    (c) at a considerable disadvantage.

7. If a man *loses his touch,* he
    (a) loses his attractiveness or influence with others.
    (b) loses all his money.
    (c) loses his sense of touch.

8. If something is *on hand,* it is
    (a) like a pair of gloves.
    (b) inaccessible.
    (c) within reach.

9. When an employee *steps down,* he
    (a) leaves an important position with his firm or company.
    (b) goes downstairs.
    (c) becomes less reliable.

10. If a football game is *rained out,* it
    (a) is called off on account of a power failure.
    (b) is postponed on account of rain.
    (c) is stopped because of the bottles thrown by the spectators.

**B.** Answer these questions, making use of the idiomatic expressions studied in this lesson.

1.  If Joe already *has two strikes against him*, is he in a favorable or unfavorable position?

2.  When a new suit of clothes *is a steal*, is it stolen from its true owner or a great bargain?

3.  If I say that I *more or less* understand you, do I definitely know what you mean or not entirely but almost know?

4.  When a baseball game is *rained out*, is it unaccompanied by rain or is it postponed on account of rain?

5.  If your pills are always *on hand* when you need them, are they near you or far away?

6.  If your test answers were *more or less* correct, did you do poorly or fairly well?

7.  Have you ever *gone off the deep end* in romance?

8.  At what age does an employee usually *step down*?

9.  Why might you feel that a new car regularly priced at $3,500 and on sale for $1,500 *is a steal*?

10. Why would an employee *play up to* his or her boss?

11. How can you tell when a magician has *lost* his *touch*?

1.  **to kick (something) around:** (to discuss in an informal way)
    1.  At first our committee didn't want to accept my plan for a proposed branch office, and so they decided to *kick* it *around for a while*.
    2.  Herb suggested that we *kick around* the treasurer's idea of insuring our employees before we hold a top-level conference on the matter.

2.  **on the ball:** (alert, attentive, competent)
    1.  We'll have to be *on the ball* in order to win this game. The other team is very good.
    2.  Ellen was certainly *on the ball* when she thought ahead and made our reservations; the rest of us had forgotten.

3.  **to say nothing of:** (without having to mention what might well be mentioned)
    1.  That employee is frequently late and also out a good deal—*to say nothing of* his laziness.

2. To *cover up* something is to
   (hide it, raise it, talk about it openly).

3. *To get into the swing of things* is to
   (swing oneself through the air, get adjusted, get tired).

4. *Things are looking up* means
   (things are looking at you, things are improving, you are looking upwards).

5. One usually tries to *pull oneself together* after
   (a good meal, after watching TV, after a crisis or bad news).

6. Someone who is *on the ball* is
   (paying attention, on the top of a football, out of the action).

7. *To get lost* is to
   (go away, be unable to find one's way, lose valuables).

8. *To drop* someone *off* means to
   (ignore her, take her some place on your way to some other place, never speak to her again).

9. When one adds to a sentence *to say nothing of* something, one means
   (to keep it quiet, to mention it, to omit mentioning it).

10. If Al *fronts for* his boss, he
    (sits in front of him, acts as the real director of a business, always walks ahead of him).

11. If Mary complained to her boss's boss, did she
    (go through channels, adopt the wrong procedure)?

12. When Susan is trying to *kick a habit*, she is trying to
    (get rid of it, indulge it, reduce it).

**B.** Answer these questions, making use of the idiomatic expressions in this lesson.

1. Are you depressed or lighthearted when things *are looking up?*

2. Is an employee who *plays up to* his superiors popular with his fellow workers?

3. Have you ever *dropped off* to sleep in the afternoon and not awakened for several hours?

4. Is a person who is *on the ball* likely to be a valuable employee or one who will soon be fired?

5. Is it easier or harder for a shy person to *get into the*

*swing of things* than it is for an outgoing person?

6. Do some people find it difficult to *pull* themselves *together* early in the morning? Why?

7. Do you like to come to a decision immediately when someone proposes a line of action, or do you like to *kick the idea around* a little first?

8. If your sales had *dropped off* what would you do to help them pick up again?

9. After an employee has been reprimanded by her boss, why is she likely to want a few minutes to *pull herself together* before she returns to her desk?

10. Is it wise to ask a favor from your boss' superior, or is it better to *go through channels?*

11. If the Brown Company *fronts for* a Mr. Williams, what do we know about Mr. Williams?

12. Does it take you a while to *pull yourself together* after you have had bad news?

13. Did you ever *cover up* something you did when you were a child?

1. to crack a book: (to read, study)
    1. Although George never *cracks a book,* he always manages to get good grades.
    2. If Lily thinks she can pass this course without *cracking a book,* she's wrong.
2. to trade in: (to exchange an old article for a new one plus a payment in cash, etc.) (S)
    1. Every fall that rich woman *trades in* her used car for a new model. The dealer usually gives her a pretty good price for her *trade-in.*
    2. I'm dissatisfied with my radio and plan to *trade* it *in.*
3. face to face: (directly confronting in direct communication)

1. She has been an admirer of the senator for years but has never met him *face to face*.
2. The defendant asked for a *face-to-face* meeting with his accuser.
3. I can no longer ignore this problem; I'm going to have to deal with it *face to face*.

4. to be with (someone): (to understand or follow another person's conversation or ideas)
   1. Now take that percentage and divide it by our fractional profit. *Are* you still *with* me?
   2. Will you please repeat that last statement? I'm not *with* you.

5. to ease (someone) out: (to discharge an employee gently, often with reasonable notice and good severance pay)
   1. When the new president took office, some members of the White House staff *were eased out*.
   2. Because those two companies merged, a number of their officers *were eased out*.

6. to knock it off: (to stop or cease doing something objectionable)
   1. When the teacher entered the classroom and saw two boys fighting, he cried: *"Knock it off!"*
   2. When his son was angrily muttering about being forbidden to use the family car, his father told him to *knock it off*.

7. it figures: (it seems likely, reasonable, or typical)
   1. "Since Jones was left in charge of the business while his boss was ill, he expects a good bonus." *"It figures."*
   2. When I told Evans that my secretary resented being passed over when raises were given, he said *it figured*.

8. to fill (one) in: (to inform, give background information)
   1. I'm supposed to meet the president of your company tomorrow. What kind of a person is she? Please *fill* me *in*.
   2. Not having been to the convention, my associate asked me *to fill* him *in*.

9. to make (one) tick: (to motivate one)
   1. If I knew what *made* my customers *tick*, I would be able to sell them more merchandise.
   2. It's difficult for us to figure out what *makes* our new boss *tick*.

10. **to cover for:** (to take charge of or assume responsibility for another person's duties or work)
    1. Go on and take your coffee break. I'll *cover for* you until you return.
    2. Allan has to go to lunch early today. Can you *cover for* him from twelve to one-thirty?

11. **to give (one) a break:** (to give another person an opportunity, chance, or forgiveness)
    1. After the police had stopped him for speeding, the driver pleaded with them *to give* him *a break* and not issue a summons.
    2. "*Give* us *a break,*" begged the students when they heard the length of the assignment. "We don't have time to do all that!"

12. **to bow out:** (to cease taking part in, remove oneself from a situation, quit)
    1. She *bowed out* as the school's registrar after 16 years of service.
    2. If we can't agree on the location, one of us is going to have to *bow out* of this partnership.

13. **to cop out:** (to retreat, withdraw from or abandon something)
    1. We expected that foundation to give our school some money, but it *copped out*.
    2. After Ellen agreed to march in our antiwar parade, why did she *cop out*?
    3. What a *copout*! Saying that you don't have the time is a poor excuse, Tony.

A. Substitute an idiomatic expression for the word or words in italics. Make any necessary changes in the form of the word in parentheses. Some substitutions may require other grammatical changes as well.

## EXERCISES

1. After the teacher had listened to the two girls arguing over the marks, she told them to *quit*.

   (knock _____)

2. Is it power or money that *motivates* him?

   (makes him _____)

3. Elsa agreed to *assume* Irma's *duties* in the office while she went shopping.

   (cover _____)

4. As I turned the corner I came *directly in front of* a police officer.

   (face _____)

5. Since the treasurer had been ill when the annual meeting took place, he later asked the secretary to *give him the details* of the meeting.

   (fill _____)

6. Although Nellie had consistently refused to go out with Paul, he pleaded with her to reconsider and *give him a chance*.

   (give him a _____)

7. Mother had promised to go to the Flower Show with us, but at the last moment she *decided not to go*.

   (_____ out)

8. "I'm sorry, the doctor can't see you today. He is so busy that he can only take care of patients who are seriously ill." *"That sounds reasonable."*

   (It _____)

9. Martha never *looks at a book* from one day to another.

   (never _____a book)

10. Yes, *I can follow the point you are making.*

    (I am with _____)

**B.** Answer these questions, making use of the idiomatic expressions studied in this lesson.

1. Have you ever had to *bow out* of a program or project before it was finished?

2. What's the difference between *to bow* and *to bow out*?

3. Who and what is the man the president just introduced us to? Can you *fill me in*?

4. What is the difference in meaning between *knock off* and *knock it off*?

5. Do you prefer discussing a problem with someone over the phone or *face to face*?

6. Who *covers for* the switchboard operator when she is out to lunch?

7. Do you sometimes wonder what *makes* a certain person *tick*, or doesn't that thought ever arise?

8. Do you ever *give* beggars *a break*, or do you pass them by?

9. How do some students pass an examination without *cracking a book*?

10. Why did Geraldine *cop out* when George called to take her swimming?

11. *Does it figure* that a happy, well-adjusted man would commit suicide?

12. What time of year is best for *trading in* a car?

13. What is the difference between *easing* an employee *out* and firing him?

14. Is a retiring employee *eased out* or is he automatically dropped from employment?

1. to pin (something) on (one): (to fix responsibility on the wrongdoer, or to transfer the blame or the guilt from the wrongdoer to someone else)
   1. During the trial, the prosecuting attorney tried *to pin* the murder *on* the victim's husband, but the jury returned a verdict of not guilty.
   2. "Who broke this window?" "I don't know, but you can't *pin* it *on* me."

2. to get a rise out of (one): (to cause resentment or confusion in another person or to provoke a retort)
   1. When I told the boss that we were losing sales to our competitor, I really *got a rise out of her.*
   2. You can kid that guy all night, but you'll never *get a rise out of him.*

*Just ignore him. He only does it to get a rise out of me.*

3. **to stick around:** (to stay or remain where one is)
   1. When our dinner guest got up to leave, we begged him *to stick around* and watch a recent movie on TV.
   2. I can't *stick around* this delightful party any longer; I have to get back to work.

4. **to pick up the tab:** (to pay for another's restaurant check, to treat another person to theater tickets, etc.)
   1. The advertising manager is flying to Puerto Rico for a conference, and his firm is *picking up the tab*.
   2. Of course our government *picks up the tab* for all the congressional junkets. The representatives don't have to pay for anything.

5. **to call it a day:** (to stop work on any activity for the day)
   1. Eileen worked hard on her biology project until 10:30 before *calling it a day*.
   2. Herb worked on his car's engine all morning, then he *called it a day* and went fishing.
   3. I don't think there'll be any more customers today. Let's *call it a day*.

6. **to go to town:** (to do something thoroughly, often successfully)
   1. Larry really *goes to town* on stage; he loses all his inhibitions.

2. Our decorator certainly *went to town* on those silk curtains. They cost a fortune.

7. to let (something) slide: (to neglect some duty) (S)
   1. I should have paid that bill promptly instead of *letting it slide*.
   2. Don't *let* your interest in our project *slide*.

8. search me: (I don't know—used informally only)
   1. "Where does that salesman go on his vacation?" "You can *search me.*"
   2. "Why does the chef always leave the restaurant with a big package?" "*Search me.*"

9. can't help (but): (be compelled to, can only, unable to avoid)
   1. I'm on a diet, but when I saw the candy, I *couldn't help but* eat a piece.
   2. When a phone rings, I *can't help but* answer it.
   3. He didn't mean to take the last one; he just *couldn't help* it.
   4. She *can't help* wanting to win—it's her competitive nature.

10. to live it up: (to live in luxury, spend freely)
    1. Let's go to Europe for two weeks and *live it up*.
    2. After getting a large inheritance, Bob and Alice *lived it up* for years.

11. to do a snow job: (to cajole or deceive another person. Also *to snow* someone)
    1. Gerald really *snowed* Brenda, and she believed every word. I hope she finds out the truth about him.
    2. That salesman who sold me this car *did a snow job* on me. It's been in the repair shop ever since I bought it.

12. to have a voice in: (to have some share, say, or direction in)
    1. The new vice-president was promised that he would *have a voice in* developing the company's international expansion.
    2. Those students are trying to get *a voice in* the administration of the college.

# EXERCISES

**A.** Find and underline the expression given in parentheses that corresponds to the italicized idiom.

1. *To go to town* is to
   (leave the country for the city, do something thoroughly, go shopping).

2. *To have a voice in* something means to
   (have a say in, be able to talk, be able to sing).

3. *To stick around* means to
   (affix stamps to package, work unsatisfactorily, remain in one place).

4. *To let* something *slide* is to
   (neglect some duty, push something over a slippery surface, permit something to be put in motion).

5. When one *picks up the tab*, one
   (makes another person's acquaintance, pays the others' bills, stoops down to get something that has been dropped).

6. If you *pin* something *on* someone, you
   (make him responsible, decorate him, label him).

7. To say that a couple certainly *lived it up* when they moved to a larger apartment and threw lots of parties means that they
   (moved upstairs, used up all their money, lived expensively).

8. *To call it a day* means to
   (quit for the day, recite the names of the days of the week, start work).

9. You are likely to *get a rise out of* another person if you
   (compliment him, insult him, work hard for him).

10. If you *can't help but* do something, you
    (won't, must, are afraid to) do it.

**B.** Answer these questions, making use of the idiomatic expressions studied in this lesson.

1. Is it a good idea to *let* your homework *slide* until the last moment, or is it better to work on it over a longer period?

2. Do you like to *stick around* after class and ask the teacher questions, or do you like to leave the classroom promptly?

3. If I *can't help* wanting a kitten, do I want it or not?

4. Do you think college students should *have a voice in* the administration of their college?

5. Do you know any cultures in which women do not *have a voice in* family finances?

6. When do you usually *call it a day* and go to bed?

7. This is a difficult lesson. Shall we *call it a day*? Why not?

8. Which type of person is it harder to *get a rise out of*—a bad-tempered individual or an even-tempered one?

9. Is a suspect likely to be convicted if the police *pin a murder charge on him*?

10. If your boss invites you to lunch, is he likely to *pick up the tab*, or are you likely to have to pay for yourself?

11. If your teacher asks you where your homework is, is it polite to answer: *"Search me"*?

12. Does it embarrass you if your friend *picks up the tab* when you are lunching together?

13. If the chairman of a reception committee *went to town* on the drinks and refreshments, would he be likely to serve champagne and caviar or beer and sandwiches?

1. to check in/out: (to register at a hotel or motel/to pay your bill at the hotel or motel and leave)
   1. Alexander *checked in* at the Plaza Hotel at 6:45 p.m. for just a brief overnight stay. He *checked out* at 9:00 a.m.
   2. *Check-out* time at most American motels is 11 a.m.
   3. The latest you can *check in* at that inn is 10 p.m. That's when they close the front desk.

2. to take (another person) at (his/or her) word: (to accept what he says as true and possibly to act on his statement)

1. I'm sorry that you want your guitar back. I *took* you *at* your *word* when you said that I could have it, and so I sold it.
2. Did you *take* your uncle *at* his *word* when he offered to buy you a car?

3. to serve (one's) purpose: (to suit one's needs or requirements, to be useful)
    1. I haven't got a screwdriver, but I think this knife will *serve* my *purpose*.
    2. My boss wanted me to interview that diplomat at his office, but I decided that a meeting in a bar would *serve* my *purpose* better.

4. in the worst way: (very much)
    1. We want to visit Italy *in the worst way*. It's our primary goal.
    2. Claudia wants to get married *in the worst way*. She spends a lot of time thinking about it.

5. to want out: (to want to be relieved of a business or social obligation, etc.)
    1. After ten years of marriage and quarreling with his wife, Jim *wants out*, so he has filed for divorce.
    2. My partner, I recently learned, is dishonest, and now I *want out* of our business.

6. to buy it: (to accept or approve of an idea, offer, or suggestion)
    1. If you offer Higgins more money than he is getting from our competitor, I'm sure he'll *buy it* and come to work for us.
    2. "Mr. President, I suggest that we offer a prize to the best typist in our office." "I'll *buy that*."

7. to line (someone or something) up: (to attain some object or goal or stand a good chance of reaching it) (S)
    1. Before the Smiths move out West, they will have to *line up* jobs there.
    2. How many votes can Senator Harkins *line up*?
    3. Rob is going to schedule the vice-president to speak at our annual convention if he can *line* him *up*.

8. to lose (one's) cool: (to get excited, flustered, or angry)
    1. Despite the disturbing hecklers in most of her audiences, Ms. Skutnik never *loses* her *cool*. She always stays calm on stage.

*Due to the accident, Randolph lost his cool.*

2. Although the group was in danger from a threatened avalanche, their guide never *lost* his *cool.*

9. to leave (something) open: (to defer decision on an offer or proposal until after further discussion)
   1. That firm is looking for a new accountant. At present the salary they will offer *has been left open.*
   2. As to your wish to have an extra secretary, let's *leave* it *open* until the next fiscal year.

10. to turn (one) on: (to greatly interest or intrigue a person. Compare: *to turn one off)*
    1. Pretty women certainly *turn* Charlie *on.*
    2. Some of the great Renaissance painters *turn* me *on,* but some of the modern ones *turn* me *off.* The pop art of the 1970s, for example, is a real *turn off* for me.

11. to miss the boat: (to lose an opportunity or to fail in some undertaking)
    1. The precious metals market often offers some very good buys, but many investors *miss the boat.*
    2. Ethan was a friend of that rich man and presumably could have been his lawyer, but somehow Ethan *missed the boat.*

12. **to dream up:** (to invent, think of and/or put into effect (S)
    1. Who *dreamed up* the idea of painting our living room walls bright red?
    2. Let's go to the automobile show and see the new car styles that Detroit has *dreamed up.*
    3. If that student didn't have a good excuse for being absent, he would *dream* one *up.*

# EXERCISES

A. Find and underline the expression given in parentheses that corresponds to the italicized idiom.

1. When Paula said, "I'll *buy that,*" she meant she would (avoid it, agree with it, contradict it).

2. *Leaving* something *open* means (deferring a decision, keeping something unclosed, departing without closing a door).

3. *To dream up* means to (guess at something, invent, awaken).

4. When one *loses* his *cool,* he gets (too warm, broke, irate).

5. When travelers *check in* to a guest house, they (sign a book, make a black mark, open an account).

6. If art *turns* Norma *on,* it (repels her, attracts her, distracts her).

7. In the *worst way* means (in the worst possible manner, very much, on the poorest route).

8. The chance of a lifetime was given George if he would only accept it, but he *missed the boat.* He (failed to act, lost a chance to get aboard a ship, longed for his boat).

9. If that partner *wants out,* he wishes to (go outdoors, leave his firm, fire an employee).

10. When the magician said that a small handkerchief from a member of the audience would *serve* his *purpose,* he meant that it would (bring his meal, be useful to him, hinder him).

11. *To take* another *at* his *word* means to
(believe him, seize him on account of his talk, listen to him).

12. *To line* something *up* is to
(draw lines around, fasten, obtain or secure something).

**B.** Answer these questions, making use of the idiomatic expressions studied in this lesson.

1. If you wanted to drink and didn't have a glass or cup, what might *serve* your *purpose?*

2. If someone insulted your mother, would you *lose* your *cool?*

3. When do you usually have to *check out* of a hotel?

4. Do you sometimes wonder where artists *dream up* their ideas?

5. Does the public *buy* these claims of the striking mailmen that they are underpaid?

6. Is Harry very much interested in Julia when he says he wants to marry her *in the worst way?*

7. What did you do when you *checked in* to that motel?

8. Have you ever *missed the boat* on a good deal? What was it?

9. Do you always *take* politicians *at their word?*

10. When a job opening is advertised, what does "salary *left open"* mean?

11. If a member of a firm says that he *wants out,* what does he want to do?

12. In what city would you like to *line up* a good job?

13. Why did someone in the income-tax department *dream up* the idea of having employers withhold part of their employees' earnings?

14. What kind of music *turns* you *on?*

# LESSON 37

1. **to throw (someone) a curve:** (to trick or mislead, embarrass or cheat)
   1. I asked them not to *throw* us any *curves*. We didn't want any surprises at the meeting.
   2. Our meeting was progressing very well until an angry employee *threw* us *a curve* by demanding that we hire more staff members.

2. **to carry on:** (a. to continue as before; b. to engage in, conduct; c. to behave in a childish, uncontrolled manner)
   a. Even in the face of certain disaster, they *carried on* as though nothing had happened.
   b. Romeo and Juliet *carried on* a secret love affair in Shakespeare's famous play.
   c. When his wife died, John cried and *carried on* so much that his family became very concerned about his health.

3. **not on your life:** (absolutely not)
   1. You want me to invest in that bankrupt company? *Not on your life!*
   2. When a friend tried to get me to learn to pilot a plane, I told him: *"Not on your life*—I'll never do that."

4. **to cover a lot of ground:** (to be extensive, to reach many decisions, to discuss several matters, etc.)
   1. That commission's report on our urban ghettos *covers a lot of ground.*
   2. In his first lecture on Plato, our philosophy teacher *covered a lot of ground.*

5. **to mind the store:** (to take care of an office, be in charge, be on duty)
   1. I have just seen most of our employees in the company cafeteria. Who is *minding the store?*
   2. Sorry I can't have lunch with you today. I'm *minding the store* while the others go and watch the St. Patrick's Day parade.

6. **to make waves:** (to create a disturbance, upset a smoothly run meeting, etc.)
   1. Before the meeting started, the committee chairman pleaded with its members not *to make waves* but to come to an agreement on the proposed law under discussion.
   2. Don't *make any waves* and you won't get into any trouble.

7. **to throw the book at:** (to be harsh, exact the full penalty)

1. Because the criminal was insulting, the judge *threw the book at* him with heavy sentences of both fines and imprisonment.
2. Remember when you were arrested for speeding, and the magistrate *threw the book at* you?

8. to clue (one) in: (to give one helpful information. Compare: *to fill one in*)
   1. I'd like you *to clue* me *in* on what happened at the last board meeting because I was absent.
   2. Before that decision relative to an increase in tuition is taken, be sure *to clue in* the trustees.

9. to be up for grabs: (to be on the open market and available to the highest bidder)
   1. Last week our florist died suddenly, and now his business *is up for grabs*.
   2. Did you know that Senator Stone is retiring and that her seat is *up for grabs*?

10. to catch up: (to bring up to date so as to finish or not be behind)
    1. I'll have to work late tonight *to catch up* on all the paperwork that's due.
    2. You've been away for months. You have a lot of *catching up* on local news to do.
    3. His years of not exercising have *caught up* with him; now he's really out of shape.

11. big deal: (very important—usually said scornfully or sarcastically)
    1. So the president to the corporation makes an annual donation of ten dollars for cancer research. *Big deal!* I'm not impressed.
    2. Elsa has been put on the reception committee of her club, so now she thinks she's a *big deal*.

A. Find and underline the expression corresponding to the italicized idiom above.

**EXERCISES**

   1. If the judge *threw the book at* a prisoner, she
      (a) hit the prisoner with a book.
      (b) read to the prisoner from a book.
      (c) gave the prisoner a harsh sentence.

2. If something is *up for grabs*, it is
    (a) available to any bidder.
    (b) higher in price.
    (c) available to thieves only.

3. When one *catches up*, she is no longer
    (a) ahead.
    (b) behind.
    (c) clumsy.

4. When someone *makes waves*, he
    (a) draws pictures of waves.
    (b) makes and transmits radio signals.
    (c) upsets an orderly discussion.

5. If one asks another to *clue* him *in*, he is requesting
    (a) information.
    (b) an invitation to come inside the other's house.
    (c) the solution of a crime.

6. *Not on your life* means
    (a) not while you are living.
    (b) never.
    (c) seldom.

7. In *covering a lot of ground*, a lecturer
    (a) walks up and down the platform.
    (b) discusses many issues or wide topics.
    (c) hides his real feelings.

8. If I *carry on* my parents' business after their death, I
    (a) continue to run it.
    (b) sell it.
    (c) make a lot of noise.

9. The expression *big deal!* conveys the idea of
    (a) pleasure or delight.
    (b) an important business transaction.
    (c) scorn or disdain.

**B.** Answer these questions, making use of the idiomatic expressions studied in this lesson.

1. In a discussion with his superior about working conditions, is an employee *making waves* when he criticizes company policy?

2. If Mr. Smith's secretary has to leave the office for a half hour, whom might she get to *mind the store*?

3. Which type of prisoner is the judge more likely *to throw the book at*—a cooperative or a disruptive one?

4. How long was it before you *caught up* on your lessons after you were out sick last week?

5. Do you think you could *carry on* a technical conversation in English?

6. In what way does an encyclopedia *cover a lot of ground*?

7. Why did Tom, after having been invited to go skiing, reply. *"Not on your life"*?

8. When you miss a class, do you find it helpful to ask a classmate *to clue* you *in*?

9. If the owner of a painting refuses to sell it, is it *up for grabs* or is it off the market?

10. If a good friend of yours suddenly slandered you, would he be *throwing* you *a curve*?

11. Are people who constantly *make waves* popular?

12. Have you *carried on* a long correspondence with anyone?

**LESSON 38**

1. to land on (one's) feet: (to recover safely from an unpleasant, risky, or dangerous situation)
   1. After a blunder that cost his company thousands of dollars, Jones *landed on* his *feet* by securing a very important contract for the firm.
   2. After all the trouble you get into, you somehow always *land on* your *feet*, don't you? How do you do it?

2. to dish out: (to distribute something, usually verbal abuse, in large quantity)
   1. That employee can't take criticism, but he can *dish* it *out*.
   2. I don't care for the sort of gossip *dished out* by your friend Gertrude.

3. to get through to (another person): (to communicate with, be understood by; also *to get to*)

1. Ames is a hard man *to get to* since he is so silent and secretive.
2. We like our new neighbors, but we can't seem *to get through to* them.
3. I'd like to get to know that deaf woman, but I can't *get through to* her, nor she to me.

4. each other/one another: (each one reciprocally, one and the other one)
   1. Doug explained that he and his wife met *each other* at a football game.
   2. When they married, they promised never to lie to *one another*.
   3. We all looked at *each other* suspiciously trying to determine who among us was the traitor.

5. to bug: (to annoy or disturb)
   1. Those neighbors of ours with their noisy radios and TV sets definitely *bug* us.
   2. We were trying to study, but Susan's daughter was constantly *bugging* us, asking for water or wanting to know when dinner would be ready.

6. to ask for: (to bring about the likelihood of something bad upon oneself)
   1. If you drink liquor and drive, you're only *asking for* trouble.
   2. Don't complain about the cut in your salary. You *asked for* it by being habitually late, absent, and inefficient.

7. to live in: (to room and sleep in the same place that one works or goes to school)
   1. Joan decided that she would *live in* for the first two years of college. She's in that dorm over there.
   2. Where can we find a cook who will *live in?*

8. to have what it takes: (to be able to act efficiently and effectively)
   1. To be a good administrator you have *to have what it takes*.
   2. Because my lawyer didn't *have what it takes*, she lost my case.

9. of course: (naturally, in the expected order of things)
   1. *Of course* I loaned her the money—she's my sister!
   2. When that country invaded our territory, we, *of course*, fought back.

10.  **to get out from under:** (to recover financially from heavy indebtedness or bankruptcy)
     1.  After severe losses sustained during the economic depression, it took most manufacturers five years *to get out from under.*
     2.  They've just doubled that storekeeper's rent. Since he is already nearly bankrupt, how can he possibly *get out from under?*

11.  **to take the bull by the horns:** (to resolutely attack a difficulty, be bold or determined)
     1.  He decided *to take the bull by the horns* and ask his boss for a raise.
     2.  After all this time, John should *take the bull by the horns* and ask Mary to marry him.

12.  **to give (one) a big hand:** (to clap one's hands in applauding a performer, or to similarly give vigorous and enthusiastic praise to a speaker, etc.)
     1.  After the vocalist had sung her number, the audience *gave* her *a* great *big hand.*
     2.  In his current review, that drama critic *gives a big hand* to a revival of <u>Hamlet</u>.

**A.** Substitute an idiomatic expression for the word or words in italics. Make any necessary changes in the form of the word in parentheses. Some substitutions may require other grammatical changes as well.

**EXERCISES**

1.  We think that Harris *has the requisite ability* to serve as dean of this school.

    (has what _____)
2.  Jane doesn't seem able *to boldly attack her problems.*

    (take the _____)
3.  Betty, who baby-sits for the Browns, has a room in their apartment where she *stays nights.*

    (lives _____)
4.  Fortunately it is easy to *communicate with* my children.

    (get _____)

5. When he is offended, Bob can *let out a voluble string of curses.*

   (dish _____)

6. Anyone who fools with an electric switch marked "danger" is *risking* trouble.

   (asking _____)

7. The voters elected Martin because they felt that he *had the necessary ability.*

   (had what _____)

8. After her *aria*, the audience *vigorously applauded* the great opera soprano.

   (gave a _____)

9. Amos has so many debts that he *will never become solvent* (recover) again.

   (get out _____)

10. Her children's constant appeals for spending money *greatly annoy her.*

    (_____ her)

11. Do you love your mother? Yes, *naturally* I do.

    (of _____)

12. Although that employee was slated to be fired, he *regained his prestige* when he received a valuable patent.

    (landed on _____)

B. Answer these questions, making use of the idiomatic expressions studied in this lesson.

   1. When one reaches safety from an embarrassing or dangerous position, does he *land on* his *feet* or land on his head?

   2. If you and your classmate were to look at *each other* right now, what would you be doing?

   3. Do members of your family look like *one another?*

   4. Does the blowing of automobile horns at night along with other traffic noises *bug* you?

   5. What kind of performer are you likely to *give a big hand* to?

6. Why does Mr. Green believe he can *get out from under* after his children graduate from college?

7. Does everyone *have what it takes* to be a doctor? Why?

8. Why would you say, *"Of course,"* if I asked you, "Are you alive?"

9. If a student neglected his homework and class attendance, wouldn't he be *asking for* a failing mark in this course?

10. Which type of student is it usually more difficult for a teacher to *get to*—an immature student or a mature one?

11. Can most radio or TV announcers *dish* it *out,* or are they inarticulate or tongue-tied?

12. What happens when a person *takes the bull by the horns?*

**LESSON 39**

1. to goof off: (to neglect one's job or duty)
   1. That stenographer is always *goofing off* in the company cafeteria instead of getting my letters typed.
   2. On Saturdays, I like to go to a movie or just *goof off* in the afternoon.

2. what with: (because of, taking into account)
   1. My elderly aunt has really suffered this winter, *what with* all the snow and cold weather we've been having.
   2. My uncle has been tired a lot lately, *what with* all the work he has to do.

3. to talk back: (to answer impertinently, to speak disrespectfully)
   1. Don't *talk back* to your parents that way; it's disrespectful.
   2. My father says that his father slapped him whenever he *talked back.*

4. to be in/out: (to be what is popular and fashionable at the time/to be no longer popular, etc.)

1.  Today at student dances, designer jeans *are in* and long skirts *are out*.
2.  It*'s in* today to be against big government.

5.  to date: (up to the present, as yet)
    1.  *To date* we've heard from 16 of the 20 people we invited.
    2.  I have not had a cold *to date* this winter.

6.  to top (something): (to surpass in wit, quality, or human interest something previously said or done)
    1.  Yesterday my car broke down, my wife had to go to the hospital, and I lost my wallet with a hundred dollars in it. Can you *top* that?
    2.  That clever TV comedian can *top* anything that anyone else on the panel says.

7.  dry run: (rehearsal)
    1.  Before we submit our plans for sales reorganization to our board of directors, let's have a *dry run* of the presentation first.
    2.  The dean called for a *dry run* of the graduation ceremonies scheduled for commencement day.

8.  to play by ear: (a. to play a piece of music that one has heard without ever having seen the music b. to act or postpone action according to what develops rather than according to a preconceived plan)
    a.  That pianist can *play* most popular tunes *by ear*. She doesn't read music.
    b.  Since matters arose at the business meeting that I hadn't been briefed on, I decided *to play* it *by ear* rather than show my ignorance by asking a lot of questions.

9.  to get (step) out of line: (to disobey, ignore, or violate orders, customs, or regulations that others accept and practice)
    1.  When Oscar reported for work drunk, his boss told him that if he ever *got out of line* again he would be fired.
    2.  *"Get out of line* just once more and I'll expel you from school," the principal told the insolent high school student.

10. fringe benefit: (something valuable that an employee gets besides wages or salary)
    1.  That Wall Street clerk gets a moderate salary, but he has several *fringe benefits* such as free lunches, life insurance, and a yearly bonus.

2. It's hard to attract employees nowadays without offering them *fringe benefits*.

11. **to fix (someone or something) up:** (a. to arrange a date or an engagement for another person. b. to repair or put something in order) (S)

   a. Since the out-of-town salesman didn't have a partner for the company dance, his friend *fixed him up* with a date.

   b. We decided to *fix* the old house *up* ourselves.

   c. His aunt was always trying to *fix* him *up* with dates with the young women in her neighborhood.

12. **to be had:** (to be victimized or cheated)

   1. "You mean these aren't real diamonds?" she exclaimed when she got home. "Oh, *I've been had!*"

   2. The angry customer complained about being overcharged at the supermarket, asserting that *he'd been had*.

**A.** Find and underline the expression given in parentheses that corresponds to the italicized idiom.

   1. *To get out of line* is to
      (leave a line one has been standing in, violate a regulation, be short of string or cord).

   2. When one says that he *has been had*, he means that he has been
      (cheated, entertained by a host, hired to do a job).

   3. To have *a dry run* is to
      (have a rehearsal, go for a run without getting wet, have a poor time financially).

   4. When one *goofs off* he
      (moves to another city, avoids or neglects his work, falls off a high place).

   5. If someone *talks back*, he or she is being
      (happy, rude, clumsy).

   6. To *fix* someone *up* is to

(ruin something, cancel a doctor's appointment, arrange a social or business date).

7. If I couldn't get to work on time *what with* the rain and my flat tire, I mean that I was late
(in spite of, because of, regardless of) those events.

8. If I say I haven't heard from them *to date*, I mean
(up to now, with a calendar, they went out together).

9. *To play* it *by ear* is to
(arrange one's hair about one's ears, watch what develops and postpone action, wiggle one's ears).

10. When a worker receives a *fringe benefit*, it is
(a very small benefit, an extra benefit besides his wages, a fixed percentage of his wages).

11. *To top* something means to
(improve on it, cover it, roof it).

12. To say capes are *in* is to assert that they are
(worn only by a select circle, worn only indoors, worn by people who wish to keep in fashion).

**B.** Answer these questions, making use of the idiomatic expressions studied in this lesson.

1. When a car bought at a great bargain proved to be a stolen one and had to be returned to its rightful owner, why did the purchaser declare that he *had been had?*

2. Did you ever *talk back* to your grandparents?

3. Would it be *out of line* for a dinner guest to propose a toast to his hostess?

4. When a prisoner *gets out of line,* what methods of discipline might a prison warden use?

5. Why did Jim ask Terry *to fix* him *up* with her roommate?

6. Why is it advisable to have a *dry run* of an advertising presentation before it is formally submitted to a client?

7. Is it *in* to dance the waltz, or is such dancing totally out of fashion today?

8. What are standard *fringe benefits* of jobs in the United States?

9. When an employee or student *goofs off*, does he make a good impression on his employer or teacher?

10. What do you think of a person who *tops* anything that you say or do?

11. What is the difference between *what* and *what with*?

12. When one is unprepared at a meeting, is it smarter *to play it by ear* than it is to confess one's ignorance and ask pertinent questions?

13. What does *play it by ear* mean when applied to performing on a musical instrument?

14. What's the longest English word you've learned *to date*?

**A.** In the blank spaces at the right, give a ONE-WORD synonym for the italicized word or words. Follow the example in the first sentence.

LESSONS 1–39

1. Joan *gets up* at seven every morning.  arises

2. Getting that $8000 car for $4500 was a *steal*.  _____

3. My young son *took part* in a school play.  _____

4. Last night's baseball game was *rained out*.  _____

5. By eleven o'clock the party *was over*.  _____

6. Before approving the new contract, my boss asked me *to fill* her *in* on the details.  _____

7. Jim and I *take turns* riding his bike.  _____

8. Tired of his fellow employee's complaints, Joe told him to *knock it off*.  _____

9. Before you take that exam, you *had better* study hard. _____

10. We thought Black was the head of that company, but he only *fronts for* Mr. Evans. _____

11. I had to *call off* that trip to the museum. _____

12. As I started to cross the busy street, someone cried: *"Look out!"* _____

13. Bill wants to *trade in* his present car for a new model. _____

14. I believe that stone was thrown through the window *on purpose*. _____

15. Let's *call it a day* and go out for a sandwich. _____

16. I *looked up* that word in my dictionary, but I couldn't find it. _____

17. Last night we *talked over* our plans for next summer. _____

18. The audience *gave a big hand to* the accomplished violinist. _____

19. At first it was hard to quit smoking, but later on I got *used to it*. _____

20. That rich man flew all his guests from New York to Los Angeles and *picked up the tab* for everything. _____

21. She's *carrying on* the business in her husband's absence. _____

22. Do you keep an extra pair of glasses *on hand* in case you break one? _____

23. Bernice's paper was so bad that her teacher asked her to *do it over*. _____

24. What did your hostess *have on* last evening? _____

25. Since the restaurant had *run out of* steak, we ordered roast beef.  _____

26. Smith hit Tom after Tom had insulted him. If you ask me, Tom had *asked for* it.  _____

27. That guest certainly knows how to *play up to* his host.  _____

28. The teacher told Alex to stop *fooling around* and start studying.  _____

29. In order to be at work on time, you must *get up* early.  _____

30. Elsa *took pains* with her appearance.  _____

**B.** Substitute in place of the italicized word or words, an idiomatic expression with *to get*. (Examples: *get out from under, get to one, get lost, get even with, get over, get through, get away with, get on one's nerves, get out of line, get in touch with, get a rise out of, get into the swing of things, get along*)

1. Jane has just *recovered* from a long illness.

2. Since we were talking privately, we told our young son to *remove himself*.

3. You can *reach* me either at home or at my office.

4. How is Lynette *progressing* in her business administration course?

5. Although he was heavily in debt, Burns finally *recovered financially*.

6. Ron *took revenge* by punching the man who insulted him.

7. After a brief training period, the new employee easily *adjusted to* his job.

8. Today's parents often find it difficult *to communicate with* their children.

9. At what time did you *finish your work* today?

10. That loud television set of our neighbor's *annoys us*.

11. Although that employee is frequently absent and usually late to the office, he *never gets any complaints*.

12. Making fun of his sister's boyfriend *provoked the retort:* "Mind your own business."

13. The boss told Ames that if he *disobeyed orders* he would be fired.

14. How is Jones *succeeding* in his business?

C. In each of the following sentences *part* of an italicized idiom is followed by a blank. From the following list of prepositions choose the one that correctly completes each idiom:

> down    in    over    through    up
> for    off    out    together    with

1. Ellen *broke* _____ her engagement because her fiancé drank too much. (terminated)

2. John just got a raise. Things *are looking* _____. (improving)

3. The chairman *turned* _____ the meeting to the principal speaker. (transferred, gave to)

4. I had counted on Jack going fishing with me, but he *backed* _____ . (refused to come)

5. After receiving an inheritance, we went to Paris and *lived it* _____ . (lived expensively)

6. Henry and his wife each *has a voice* _____ the family business. (a share)

7. Mother is planning *to take* _____ painting this winter. (start)

8. We couldn't get our car up the hill—*what* _____ all the extra weight.

9. That plane is *bound* _____ Rome. (has Rome as its destination)

10. Roger wanted to go out with Edith, but she *turned* him _____ . (rejected him)

D. Match the idiom in column I with the definition in column II.

| I | II |
|---|---|
| 1. put up with __g__ | a. immediately |
| 2. of course _____ | b. distribute |
| 3. take turns _____ | c. as yet |

4. go through _____       d. leave
5. get even with _____    e. alternate
6. to date _____          f. discuss informally
7. take off _____         g. tolerate
8. at once _____          h. experience
9. goof off _____         i. be careful
10. kick around _____     j. neglect one's job
11. look out _____        k. naturally
12. pass out _____        l. retaliate

**E.** In the space provided, mark whether the sentences are true (T) or false (F).

1. If you *hang up* a telephone, you call your best friend. _____

2. If you have a *dry run* of something, you rehearse it. _____

3. If you and your friend share the prize money *fifty-fifty*, it means that you get more than she does. _____

4. If you *back* your car *up*, you have put the gears into reverse. _____

5. If you were *brought up* in Buenos Aires, you were raised there. _____

6. If you *bow out* of a situation, you stop participating. _____

7. If you *are into* chess, it means you hate the game. _____

8. If you say, "Let's *call it a day*," it means you want to continue working for a while. _____

9. If you have a *face-to-face* confrontation, you are probably talking on the telephone. _____

10. If you *pull off* a good trick on your best friend, it means you fail. _____

# APPENDIX
# I

A Note on
Separable Idioms

## Type I.

In English, certain idioms among those of the "two-word verb" class are *separable* by their direct object or complement; that is, the *pronoun* direct object is placed between the verb and its accompanying prepositional particle. For example, in speaking of turning off the lights, we can say: **John** *put them out.* Less frequently among the group of separable idioms we can similarly insert a *noun* direct object, as in: **John** *put the lights out,* which has the same meaning as **John** *put out the lights.* Note that the *pronoun* direct object never appears *after* the particle of a separable idiom as it often does after a non-separable idiom. For example, it is wrong to say: **John** *put out it* instead of **John** *put it out;* but we can say: **The firm** *got rid of her,* since *get rid of* is inseparable.

In *Essential Idioms* we have placed the symbol (S) after the definitions of those terms that are separable and have provided illustrative variations in word order. No satisfactory rule has been found that will indicate which idioms are separable and which are not. In this book it happens that the great majority of two-word idioms using the particles *out* and *up* are separable. Also one can find some, but fewer, examples of the particles *down, off,* and *over* that may be split from their verbs by a pronoun direct object.

## Type II.

It should be noted here that some idioms that do not take a direct object may be split by an adjective or adverb. For example: **Unable to keep up with the adults on the long walk, the child** *fell far behind* (fell behind); **The student** *paid strict attention to* **the teacher** (paid attention to). However, these insertions of *far* and *strict* differ from the splitting of an idiom by a direct object, since they *qualify* the sense of the sentences written without them. In *Essential Idioms*, Type II separable idioms have not been labeled, but their use is sometimes revealed in the illustrative sentences.

# APPENDIX II

| Lesson 1 | *Spanish* | *French* | *German* |
|---|---|---|---|
| to get on | subirse, montarse | monter | einsteigen |
| to get off | bajarse, apearse | descendre, sortir | aussteigen |
| to put on | ponerse | mettre | aufsetzen, anziehen |
| to take off | quitarse | enlever | ausziehen |
| to call up | llamar (por teléfono) | téléphoner, un coup de fil | anrufen |
| to turn on | encender, abrir | allumer, ouvrir | anmachen, andrehen |
| to turn off | apagar, cerrar | éteindre, fermer | ausmachen, ausdrehen |
| right away | inmediatamente | immédiatement | sofort |
| to pick up | tomar, coger | ramasser, prendre | aufheben |
| at once | enseguida, inmedia-tamente | tout de suite | sofort, gleich |
| to get up | levantarse | se lever | aufstehen |
| at first | al principio | au premier abord | zuerst |

| Lesson 2 | | | |
|---|---|---|---|
| to wait for | aguardar | attendre | warten auf |
| at last | por fin | enfin | endlich |
| as usual | como de costumbre | comme d'habitude | wie gewöhnlich |
| to find out | averiguar | trouver, découvrir | feststellen, ausfinden |
| to look at | mirar, contemplar | regarder, envisager | ansehen, anschauen |
| to look for | buscar, indagar | chercher, rechercher | suchen |
| all right | satisfactorio | c'est bien | zufrieden sein, richtig |
| right here | aquí mismo | ici-même | genau hier |
| little by little | poco a poco, lentamente | au fur et à mesure | nach und nach |
| tired out | exhausto, agotado | n'en pouvoir plus | übermüdet |
| to call on | visitar | visiter | besuchen |
| never mind | no se preocupe, no importa | peu importe | schon gut |

| Lesson 3 | *Spanish* | *French* | *German* |
|---|---|---|---|
| to pick out | seleccionar, escoger | choisir | aussuchen |
| to take (one's) time | tomarse su tiempo, proceder con calma | prendre son temps | Zeit nehmen |
| to talk over | discutir | discuter | besprechen |
| to lie down | acostarse | s'étendre | sich hinlegen |
| to stand up | ponerse de pie | se mettre debout | aufstehen |
| to sit down | sentarse | s'asseoir | sich hinsetzen |
| all day | todo el día | toute la journée | den ganzen Tag |
| by oneself | por sí mismo, solo | tout seul | alleine |
| on purpose | a propósito, adrede | exprès | absichtlich |
| to get along | irle bien o mal | s'entendre, faire des progrès | auskommen |
| to make no difference | dar lo mismo, ser igual | être égal | keinen Unterschied machen |
| to take out | sacar, extraer | sortir | herausnehmen |

| Lesson 4 | | | |
|---|---|---|---|
| to take part | tomar parte, participar | participer à | teilnehmen |
| at all | de ninguna manera | du tout | überhaupt nicht |
| to look up | indagar, buscar | chercher | nachschauen |
| to wait on | depachar, servir | servir | bedienen |
| at least | por lo menos | au moins | wenigstens |
| so far | hasta ahora | jusqu'à présent | bis jetzt |
| to take a walk | dar un paseo a pie | faire une promenade | Spaziergang machen |
| to take a seat | tomar asiento, sentarse | prendre un siège | platznehmen |
| to try on | probarse | essayer | anprobieren |
| to think over | reflexionar, meditar | réfléchir | überlegen |
| to take place | suceder, ocurrir | avoir lieu | stattfinden |
| to put away | guardar, recoger | ranger | weglegen |
| to look out | tener cuidado | prendre garde | aufpassen |
| to shake hands | dar la mano | serrer la main, donner une poignée de main | Hand reichen |

## Lesson 5

| | | | |
|---|---|---|---|
| to think of | parecerle a uno, opinar | penser à | davon halten, Meinung haben |
| to get back | regresar | revenir, retourner | zurückkommen |
| to catch cold | resfriarse, acatarrarse | prendre froid | sich erkälten |
| to make up (one's) mind | decidirse | se décider | sich entschliessen |
| to change (one's) mind | cambiar de opinión o idea | changer d'idée, changer d'avis | Meinung ändern |
| for the time being | por ahora, mientras tanto | pour le moment | zur Zeit |
| to get over | reponerse, restablecerse | se consoler, se remettre | hinwegkommen |
| to call off | cancelar | annuler | absagen |
| for good | para siempre, permanente- mente | pour de bon | für immer, ständig |
| in a hurry | rápidamente | être pressé | in Eile |

## Lesson 6

| | | | |
|---|---|---|---|
| to hang up | colgar | suspendre, raccrocher (téléphone) | aufhängen |
| according to | de acuerdo con | selon | gemäss |
| to count on | contar con | compter sur | rechnen auf |
| to make friends | hacer amigos | faire des amis | Freundschaft anschliessen |
| out of order | descompuesto | ne pas fonctionner | ausser Betrieb |
| to get to | llegar a | arriver à | ankommen |
| at times | a veces | quelquefois, parfois | gelengentlich |
| to look over | revisar, examinar | examiner, vérifier | prüfen, nachsehen |
| to have time off | tener tiempo libre | avoir du temps libre | frei haben |
| to keep on | continuar | continuer à | fortfahren |
| to put out | sofocar, apagar, extinguir | éteindre | auslöschen, ausmachen |
| all of a sudden | súbitamente, repentina- mente, de pronto | tout à coup | plötzlich |

| Lesson 7 | Spanish | French | German |
|---|---|---|---|
| to point out | señalar, mostrar | signaler, montrer du doigt | bezeichnen, anmerken |
| to be over | haber terminado | être fini | vorüber sein |
| to be up | llegar la hora | être terminé | beenden |
| on time | a la hora indicada | à l'heure, à temps | pünktlich sein |
| in time | a tiempo, antes de la hora indicada | à temps | zur Zeit |
| to get better | mejorar | aller mieux, s'améliorer | besser werden |
| to get sick | enfermarse | tomber malade | krank werden |
| had better | es mejor que | il vaut mieux que | für besser halten |
| would rather | preferir | préférer | vorzichen |
| by the way | a propósito | à propos | nebenbei |
| to figure out | razonar, entender | imaginer, calculer | herausfinden |
| to put off | aplazar, posponer | remettre | aufschieben |

| Lesson 8 | | | |
|---|---|---|---|
| to be about to | estar a punto de | être sur le point de | im Begriff sein |
| to turn around | dar la vuelta | se retourner | umdrehen |
| to take turns | alternar | alterner | abwechseln |
| to pay attention | prestar atención | faire attention | aufpassen |
| to go on | seguir, continuar | continuer | fortfahren |
| over and over | repetidamente | sans cesse | immer wieder |
| to wear out | gastarse | user | abgetragen, abgenutzt |
| to throw away | botar, echar | jeter | wegwerfen |
| to fall in love | enamorarse | tomber amoureux | sich verlieben |
| to go out | apagarse, salir | sortir, s'éteindre | ausgehen |
| as yet | hasta ahora | jusqu'à présent | bis jetzt |
| to have to do with | tener que ver con | y être pour quelque chose | zu tun haben mit |

| Lesson 9 | | | |
|---|---|---|---|
| to wake up | despertarse | s'éveiller, se réveiller | aufwachen |
| to be in charge of | estar a cargo de | être chargé de | Sorge tragen für |
| as soon as | tan pronto como | aussitôt que | so bald als |
| to get in touch with | communicarse con | communiquer avec | in Verbindung treten |
| to have a good time | divertirse | bien s'amuser | sich amüsieren |

| | Spanish | French | German |
|---|---|---|---|
| to take care of | ocuparse de, cuidar de | prendre soin de | sorgen dafür, pflegen |
| once in a while | de vez en cuando | de temps en temps | gelegentlich, von Zeit zu Zeit |
| quite a few | muchos | pas mal de | einige |
| used to | acostumbraba | avoir l'habitude de | früher gewöhnt sein an |
| to be used to | estar acostumbrado a | être accoutumé à, avoir l'habitude de | Angewohnheit haben |
| to get used to | acostumbrarse a | s'accoutumer à | sich einstellen auf |
| back and forth | de un lado para otro | va-et-vient | hin und her |

**Lesson 10**

| | Spanish | French | German |
|---|---|---|---|
| to make sure | asegurar, garantizar | s'assurer de | sicher machen |
| now and then | de vez en cuando | de temps en temps | von Zeit zu Zeit |
| to make out | irle bien, salir bien | réussir | Erfolg haben |
| who's who | quien es importante | qui fait quoi | wer ist was |
| to go with | hacer juego | s'accorder | mitgehen |
| to go with | ir con, salir con | fréquenter, sortir avec | zusammen ausgehen |
| to come from | proceder de | venir de (quelque part) | herkommen |
| to make good time | viajar rápidamente | voyager vite, bien marcher (train) | schnelle Fahrt haben |
| to mix up | equivocar, mezclar, confundir | s'embrouiller | durcheinander bringen |
| to see about | ocuparse de | s'occuper de | nachsehen |
| to get rid of | deshacerse de | se défaire de, se débarasser de | loswerden |
| by heart | de memoria | par cœur | auswendig |

**Lesson 11**

| | Spanish | French | German |
|---|---|---|---|
| to keep out | no entrar | défendre d'entrer | fernhalten |
| to find fault with | criticar | trouver à redire | kritisieren |
| to be up to someone | depender de alguien | dépendre de | abhängen von |
| off and on | de vez en cuando | de temps à autre | gelegentlich |
| to catch fire | coger fuego, incendiarse | prendre feu | Feuer fangen |

|  | Spanish | French | German |
|---|---|---|---|
| to look into | investigar | examiner attentivement | prüfen |
| to take hold of | agarrarse de | saisir | anfassen |
| to be out of the question | ser imposible | être absolument impossible | unmöglich sein |
| to get through | terminar, acabar | terminer | beenden |
| all at once | repentinamente, de pronto | tout à coup | ganz auf einmal |
| to keep track of | llevar cuenta de | enregistrer, tenir un registre | aufzeichnen, aufschreiben |
| to get carried away | excederse | se laisser emporter | überreagieren |

| **Lesson 12** | *Spanish* | *French* | *German* |
|---|---|---|---|
| up to date | moderno, al día, al corriente | tenir à jour | neuzeitlich |
| out of date | anticuado, antiguo, arcaico | démodé, périmé, dépassé | ausser Mode |
| to blow up | explotar, volar | faire sauter, exploser | explodieren |
| to do over | rehacer | refaire | wiederholen |
| to burn down | quemarse (un edificio) | détruire par le feu | abbrennen |
| to burn up | quemarse | brûler entièrement | verbrennen |
| to burn out | fundirse | brûler | ausbrennen |
| to make good | tener éxito | réussir | Erfolg haben |
| it stand to reason | ser natural, lógico | il va sans dire | ohne Zweifel |
| to break out | estallar, comenzar súbitamente | éclater | ausbrechen |
| as to | en cuanto a | en tant que, quant à | was anbetrifft |
| to feel sorry for | tener lástima de | avoir pitié de | Mitleid haben |
| to take (something) for granted | dar por descontado | être persuadé | selbstverständlich halten |

| **Lesson 13** |  |  |  |
|---|---|---|---|
| to break down | romperse | ne plus marcher | versagen |
| to turn out | resultar | finalement devenir | herausdrehen |
| to become of | sucederle, hacerse de | advenir | sich ereignen |

|  | Spanish | French | German |
|---|---|---|---|
| to give up | dejar de, reindirse | se rendre, abdiquer, abandonner | aufgeben, passieren |
| to take pity on | tener lástima de | avoir pitié de | Mit leid haben |
| to cross out | tachar | barrer | ausstreichen |
| to take into account | tener en cuenta, tener en consideración | tenir compte de | in Betracht ziehen |
| to make clear | aclarar | clarifier | erklären |
| to take a look at | mirar a | jeter un coup d'œil | ansehen |
| to have on | tener puesto | porter | tragen |
| to come to | volver en sí | revenir à soi, se remettre | zu sich kommen |
| to call for | ir a buscar | venir chercher | abholen |

**Lesson 14**

|  | Spanish | French | German |
|---|---|---|---|
| to eat in/to eat out | comer en casa/ comer fuera | manger à la maison, au restaurant | zu Hause essen, ausessen |
| to play tricks on | tomarle el pelo a | jouer un tour à quelqu'un | Schabernack spielen |
| to look after | cuidar de | s'occuper de | aufpassen |
| to feel like | tener ganas de | avoir envie de | Lust haben |
| once and for all | de una vez y para siempre | une fois pour toutes | endgültig |
| to hear from | recibir noticias de, saber de | recevoir des nouvelles | Nachricht bekommen |
| to hear of | oír hablar de, saber de | entendre parler de | etwas hören von, über |
| to make fun of | burlarse de | se moquer de, se rire de | sich lustig machen |
| to come true | resultar cierto | devenir un fait accompli | wahr werden |
| as a matter of fact | en realidad, es más | le fait est que | tatsächlich Kopf gehen |
| to have (one's) way | salirse con la suya | en faire à sa tête | mit Freude oder Ungeduld erwarten |
| to look forward to | aguardar con ansia | attendre avec impatience | nach dem eigenen |

**Lesson 15**

|  | Spanish | French | German |
|---|---|---|---|
| inside out/ upside down | al revés, boca abajo | sens dessus, dessous | Innenseite nach aussen, umgedreht |
| to fill out | llenar | remplir | ausfüllen |

|  | *Spanish* | *French* | *German* |
|---|---|---|---|
| to take advantage of | aprovecharse de | profiter de | ausnützen |
| no matter | no importa | n'importe | ohne auf etwas zu achten |
| to take up | estudiar | étudier | studieren, belegen |
| to take (something) up with | consultar con | discuter avec | besprechen |
| to take after | salir a | tenir de | sich ähnlich sein |
| in the long run | a la larga | à la longue | zum Schluss, am Ende |
| out of | sin | manquer de | veraltet |
| to run out of | acabarse, agotarse | manquer de | ohne Vorrat sein |

**Lesson 16**

|  | | | |
|---|---|---|---|
| every so often | de vez en cuando | assez souvent | gelegentlich |
| to get along with | llevarse bien con | s'entendre | zusammen auskommen |
| hard of hearing | medio sordo | sourd d'oreille | schlecht hörig sein |
| to let go of | soltar | lâcher | freilassen, gehenlassen |
| to keep in mind | recordar | se rappeler de | nicht vergessen |
| to run over | arrollar, atropellar | écraser | überfahren |
| to keep an eye on | vigilar | surveiller | aufpassen |
| to go off | disparar, explotar, salir de pronto | faire explosion, partir | losgehen |
| to grow out of | quitársele | passer | auswachsen |
| to make the best of | sacar el mejor partido posible | tirer le meilleur parti de | das Beste aus etwas machen |
| to cut off | cortar | couper, interrompre | abschneiden |
| to cut out | recortar | découper, cesser de, cesser immédiate-ment | ausschneiden |

| **Lesson 17** | *Spanish* | *French* | *German* |
|---|---|---|---|
| to blow out | reventarse | avoir une crevaison | platzen, explodieren |
| to shut off | apagar, cerrar | fermer, couper | abstellen |
| to shut up | cerrar, callarse | mettre les verrous, se taire | abschliessen, Mund halten |

|  | *Spanish* | *French* | *German* |
|---|---|---|---|
| to have got | tener, poseer | avoir | bekommen, besitzen |
| to have got to (do something) | tener que hacer algo | devoir | etwas tun müssen |
| to keep up with | mantenerse a la par de | aller aussi vite que | Schritt halten |
| to tell time | decir la hora | dire l'heure | die Zeit kennen |
| to turn down | rechazar | baisser, refuser | schwächer stellen, ablehnen |
| fifty-fifty | a la mitad | moitié moitié | fünfzig zu fünfzig |
| to break in | estrenar, ajustar, domar | assouplir, roder | eintragen, einfahren (car) |
| to break into | entrar en, asaltar | s'introduire | einbrechen |
| above all | sobre todo | par-dessus tout | hauptsächlich, über alles |

**Lesson 18**

|  |  |  |  |
|---|---|---|---|
| to do without | prescindir de | se passer de | ohne etwas auskommen |
| to watch out for | tener cuidado (con, de) | faire attention à | |
| to be bound to | ser inevitable | être certain de | aufpassen |
| for sure | de seguro | vraiment | ziemlich sicher |
| to take (someone) for | tomar a uno por | prendre quelqu'un pour | hingehen, hinfahren |
| to try out | probar | essayer | jemanden halten für |
| to tear down | derribar, demoler | démolir | ausprobieren |
| to tear up | rasgar, lacerar | déchirer | abreissen |
| to cut up | cortar en pedazos | couper en petits morceaux | zerreissen |
| to burn up | quemarse | consumer | abschneiden, abbrechen zerschneiden verbrennen |

**Lesson 19**

|  |  |  |  |
|---|---|---|---|
| to cut off | cortar parte de algo | couper | abschneiden |
| to tell (two things or two persons) apart | distinguir entre | distinguer entre | unterscheiden |
| all in all | teniendo todo en consideración | tous comptes faits | im ganzen |
| to pass out | desmayarse | perdre conscience | stockbesaffen |

| | Spanish | French | German |
|---|---|---|---|
| to go around | alcanzar para todos | suffire à tout le monde | herumgehen, herumreichen |
| to be in the way | estorbar | être de trop | im Wege sein |
| in vain | en vano | en vain | vergeblich, vergebens |
| to put up | construir, edificar | construire, ériger | errichten, aufbauen |
| to put up with | tolerar, soportar | tolérer | ertragen, aushalten |
| to put on weight | ganar peso | engraisser | zunehmen |
| day in, day out | a diario, día tras día | à longueur de journée | Tag ein und Tag aus |
| to show off | jactarse, presumir, ostentar | faire parade de, poseur | sich zeigen, prahlen |

**Lesson 20**

| | | | |
|---|---|---|---|
| to hold still | estarse quieto | rester tranquille | stillhalten |
| to know by sight | conocer de vista | connaître de vue | von Ansehen kennen |
| something the matter | algo le pasa | rien de déréglé, y avoir quelque chose | etwas nicht in Ordnung sein |
| to bring up | criar; presentar | élever | erziehen |
| to get lost | perderse | se perdre | sich verirren |
| to hold up | asaltar; demorar | arrêter la circulation, s'emparer de, saisir, assaillir | überfallen |
| to run away | huir, escaparse | se sauver, s'échapper | weglaufen, wegrennen |
| to rule out | descartar | éliminer | ausschliessen |
| to see someone off | despedirse de alguien | voir partir quelqu'un | Abschied nehmen |
| to set fire to | prenderle fuego a | mettre le feu à | in Brand setzen, anzünden |

**Lesson 21**

| | | | |
|---|---|---|---|
| to drive up to | ir hasta, llegar hasta, aproximarse a | conduire à, aller à, courir à | hinfahren, hinlaufen, hingehen |
| to hand in | presentar, entregar | remettre, donner | einreichen |
| in case | por si acaso | au cas où | im Falle |
| to hold on | aguantar, agarrarse, detener | saisir, tenir, arrêter, Ne quittez pas! | anhalten, aufhalten |

|  | *Spanish* | *French* | *German* |
|---|---|---|---|
| to think up | idear | inventer, imaginer | ausdenken |
| to be better off | irle mejor | valoir mieux | besser dran sein |
| to be well-off | ser de buena posición económica | dans l'aisance | vermögend sein |
| to take (someone) by surprise | sorprender a alguien | prendre au dépourvu | überraschen |
| to keep in touch with | mantenerse en contacto con | continuer à communiquer avec | in Verbindung bleiben |
| to be named after | llamarlo como | être nommé d'après | nach jemanden benannt sein |
| to put together | armar | assembler | zusammen setzen |
| to take apart | desarmar | démonter | ausein-andernehmen |

## Lesson 22

|  | *Spanish* | *French* | *German* |
|---|---|---|---|
| to give (someone) a call | llamar por teléfono a alguien | donner un coup de téléphone à | anrufen, telefonieren |
| to drop (someone) a line | escribirle unas líneas a alguien | écrire un mot | jemandem ein paar Worte schreiben |
| to come across | encontrarse con | trouver par hasard | treffen, herausfinden |
| to stand for | aguantar a; representar | représenter, tolérer | darstellen, sich gefallen lassen |
| to stand a chance | tener probabilidad | avoir la chance de | eine Möglichkeit haben |
| to make faces | hacer muecas | faire des grimaces | ein Gesicht ziehen |
| to take pains | esmerarse | prendre de la peine | etwas sorgfältig tun, sich Mühe geben |
| to look up to | admirar | avoir un grand respect pour | bewundern, respektieren |
| to look down on | despreciar | regarder de haut en bas | herabsehen auf |
| to take off | despegar | décoller | abfliegen (abhauen) |
| to pull off | lograr | réussir | fertigbringen |
| to keep good time | andar bien (un reloj) | être à l'heure | genau gehen |

| Lesson 23 | *Spanish* | *French* | *German* |
|---|---|---|---|
| to make do | improvisar | se débrouiller | auskommen |
| to give birth to | dar a luz | donner naissance à, mettre au monde | zur Welt bringen |
| to taste of | saber a | avoir le goût de | schmecken nach |
| to get on (one's) nerves | ponerlo a uno nervioso | porter sur les nerfs | nervös machen, auf die Nerven gehen |
| to put down | dominar | déposer | niederwerfen, niederdrücken |
| to go in for | ser aficionado a | s'adonner à | etwas gern haben, Freude daran haben |
| to stay up | acostarse tarde | veiller | aufbleiben |
| to stay in/to stay out | quedarse en casa; quedarse fuera de casa | rester à la maison, ne pas rentrer | zu Hause bleiben, ausbleiben |
| to be into | estar dedicado de | se passionner pour | verwickelt sein |
| to take over | encargarse de | se charger de | ubernehmen |
| to show up | presentarse, aparecerse | se présenter | sich zeigen |
| to clean out | limpiar | nettoyer (à fond) | sauber machen, reinigen |

| Lesson 24 | | | |
|---|---|---|---|
| to knock out | hacer perder el sentido de un golpe | faire perdre connaissance par un coup | jemanden bewusstlos machen, niederwerfen |
| to carry out | llevar a cabo | exécuter | ausführen |
| to run into | encontrarse con | rencontrer par hasard | unerwartet treffen |
| to set out | salir a, empezar a | se mettre en chemin | losgehen |
| to draw up | preparar | préparer | ausfüllen |
| to drop in | visitar | visiter à l'imprévu | unerwartet besuchen |
| to drop out | dejar de asistir | quitter | verlassen |
| to believe in | creer en | croire à | glauben an |
| to cheer up | alegrarse, animarse | rendre courage, réjouir | aufmuntern |
| to make sense | ser razonable, tener sentido | être logique | verständig sein |
| to blow down | echar al suelo | abattre | ausblasen, wegblasen |
| to break down | romper | enfoncer, s'évader, se détacher | durchbrechen, ausbrechen |

| Lesson 25 | *Spanish* | *French* | *German* |
|---|---|---|---|
| to burst out crying/to burst out laughing | romper a llorar/ romper a reír | éclater en sanglots, éclater de rire | zu weinen anfangen, zu lachen anfangen |
| to get away | escapar, huir | s'échapper, s'enfuir | loskommen |
| to get away with | salirse con la suya | s'en tirer | mit etwas wegkommen |
| to keep up | mantener el mismo paso | continuer au même pas, maintenir | beibehalten |
| to make up | compensar, reconciliarse, inventar | se rattraper, refaire, inventer, se maquiller | gutmachen, zurechtmachen (Gesicht) |
| to stand out | sobresalir | se distinguer de | auffallend sein, hervorstehen |
| to go wrong | salir mal | marcher mal, ne pas marcher | falsch gehen |
| to serve one right | merecer | mériter | recht geschehen |
| to let on | dejar entrever, revelar | révéler à | wissen lassen |
| to meet someone halfway | llegar a un acuerdo | faire des concessions | auf halbem Wege treffen |
| to check up | revisar, comprobar | vérifier, examiner | nachprüfen, untersuchen |
| to stick up | sobresalir | ressortir | herausstecken |

| Lesson 26 | | | |
|---|---|---|---|
| to come about | suceder, ocurrir | se produire | sich ereignen |
| to build up | aumentar | se fortifier, renforcer | auffrischen, aufbauen |
| to bring about | causar | causer, provoquer | verursachen |
| to die down | acabarse, apagarse | se calmer, s'éteindre | nachlassen, verringern |
| to fade away | desaparecer poco a poco | décroître peu à peu | abklingen |
| to die out | desaparecer | disparaître | aussterben |
| to make out | hacer, entender, preparar | déchiffrer, rédiger, réussir, comprendre, prétendre | ausschreiben, ausfinden, Resultat haben |
| to live up to | cumplir, realizar | être à la hauteur de | erreichen, erfüllen |
| to stand up for | salir en defensa de | défendre | eintreten für, sich einsetzen |

|  | *Spanish* | *French* | *German* |
| --- | --- | --- | --- |
| to stick to | defender, mantener firme | persévérer | aushalten, beharren |
| to stick (someone) | engañar, estafar | tromper, voler | übers Ohr hauen, begaunern |
| to get stuck | estafado | être volé | beschwindeln |

**Lesson 27**

|  | | | |
| --- | --- | --- | --- |
| to take on | emplear | employer, engager | einstellen, engagieren |
| to take down | descolgar, bajar, tomar nota de | décrocher, prendre note de | herunternehmen, aufschreiben |
| to fall off | caerse de, disminuir | tomber de | herunterfallen |
| to fall through | fracasar | échouer | durchfallen |
| to fall behind | atrasarse | être en retard, en arrière | zurück bleiben |
| to give in | darse por vencido, rendirse | se rendre à | nachgeben |
| to give off | producir, despedir | produire, exhaler | abgeben |
| to give out | repartir, acabarse | distribuer, être épuisé | ausgeben, verteilen |
| to have it in for | tenérselas juradas a uno, tenerla cogida con uno | en vouloir à quelqu'un | Abneigung haben |
| to have it out with | poner las cosas en claro, ventilar un asunto con alguien | régler quelque chose | ausfechten |
| to hold off | aguantar, aplazar | cesser, s'arrêter, retenir, retarder | anhalten, andauern |
| to hold out | resistir, durar | durer, être suffisant, résister | aushalten, ausreichen |
| to hold over | mantener, posponer | continuer à montrer | verlegen |
| to turn over | volcar, trasladar | se retourner, transférer | umdrehen, übergehen |

| Lesson 28 | *Spanish* | *French* | *German* |
|-----------|-----------|----------|----------|
| to let up | disminuir | diminuer, cesser | nachlassen |
| to lay off | dejar cesante, despedir | mettre au chômage | entlassen, ablegen |
| to bring out | sacar, presentar | présenter, faire paraître | hervorbringen |
| to bring back | devolver | rapporter | zurückbringen |
| to wait up for | esperar por, desvelarse en espera de | attendre | auf jemanden warten |
| to let (someone or something) alone | dejar tranquilo a | laisser tranquille | alleine lassen |
| let alone | sin mencionar | encore moins | geschweige denn |
| to break off | terminar, finalizar | rompre avec | abbrechen |
| to wear off | pasar, desaparecer poco a poco | disparaître (peu à peu) | verschwinden, aufhören |
| to wear down | gastar | user complètement | abtreten, abnützen, ausnützen |
| on the whole | en general | en somme, à tout prendre | im Allgemeinen |
| to read over | echar una ojeada | relire, jeter un coup d'œil | nachlesen, nachprüfen, überblicken |

| Lesson 29 | | | |
|-----------|-----------|----------|----------|
| to work out | planear, resultar | bien finir, deviser | ausarbeiten |
| to back up | dar marcha atrás | faire marche arrière | zurücksetzen |
| to back out | retirarse de, decidir lo contrario | changer d'avis | die Meinung ändern, sich zurückziehen |
| to be set to (do something) | estar listo para hacer algo | être prêt à faire quelque chose | bereit sein |
| to sit in | participar | assister à | anwesend sein |
| to have (one's) heart set on | anhelar, ansiar | avoir envie de, tenir à | Wunsch haben |
| to buy up | adquirir, acaparar | faire l'achat total | aufkaufen |
| to buy out | comprar la parte de | acheter la part de | auszahlen, ankaufen |
| to sell out | vender, liquidar | liquider | ausverkaufen |
| to catch on | darse cuenta, entender | y être, comprendre | verstehen, begreifen |
| to be cut out for | tener talento para | avoir l'étoffe de | veranlagt sein |
| to throw out | echar, botar | jeter à la porte, rejeter | herauswerfen |

|  | *Spanish* | *French* | *German* |
| --- | --- | --- | --- |
| to throw up | vomitar | vomir | sich übergeben |
| to clear up | aclarar, solucionar, resolver | s'éclaircir, clarifier, résoudre | auferklären |

## Lesson 30

|  | *Spanish* | *French* | *German* |
| --- | --- | --- | --- |
| to slow down | ir más despacio | ralentir | langsamer werden |
| to dry up | secarse completamente | sécher | auftrocknen |
| to dry out | secarse poco a poco | dessécher | austrocknen |
| to be up to (something) | tener algo entre manos | machiner, combiner | planen, beabsichtigen, vorhaben |
| to beat around the bush | andarse con rodeos | tourner autour du pot | indirekt sprechen |
| to come to an end | terminar, acabarse | se terminer | beenden, zum Ende bringen |
| to put an end to | darle fin a | faire cesser quelque chose | Schluss machen |
| to get even with | vengarse | se venger, rendre la pareille à | sich revanchieren |
| to fool around | perder el tiempo, bromear | perdre son temps | Unsinn machen |
| to look out on | dar a | donner sur | Aussicht haben auf |
| to stir up | provocar, incitar | exciter, pousser à, agiter | aufhetzen |
| to take in | escuchar | voir | besuchen |

## Lesson 31

|  | *Spanish* | *French* | *German* |
| --- | --- | --- | --- |
| to go through | llevar a cabo, aprobarse | souffrir, subir, aller jusqu'au bout | durchmachen |
| to go without saying | estar sobreentendido | il va sans dire que | ohne Zweifel, es muss nicht extra betönt werden |
| to put (someone) on | bromear | faire marcher quelqu'un | hintergehen |
| to keep (one's) head | mantener la calma | garder son sang-froid | den Kopf behalten |
| to lose (one's) head | perder la cabeza | perdre la tête | den Kopf verlieren |
| to cut in | interrumpir, cortar el paso | interrompre, couper en travers | unterbrechen, in den Weg kommen |

| | Spanish | French | German |
|---|---|---|---|
| to cut short | adelantar, reducir | couper court | abschneiden, abkürtzen |
| to stand up | durar; quedar mal | faire bon usage, résister, poser un lapin | halten, aufsitzen lassen |
| to get the better of | aventajar | l'emporter sur | Überhand gewinnen |
| to break loose | soltarse, zafarse | se détacher de, s'échapper, s'évader | losbrechen, ausbrechen |
| to waste one's breath | perder el tiempo | perdre son temps | Wörter ohne Ergebnis verschwenden |
| to make room for | hacerle lugar, acomodar | faire place à | Platz machen |

**Lesson 32**

| | Spanish | French | German |
|---|---|---|---|
| to have two strikes against (one) | tener las de perder | avoir deux coups contre | in einer schlechter Lage zu sein |
| to step down | retirarse, renunciar | démissionner | eine Stellung aufgeben |
| more or less | más o menos | plus ou moins | mehr oder weniger |
| to be a steal | ser una ganga | être une occasion | billig sein |
| to play up to | dar coba, adular | flatter | jemanden schmeicheln |
| to screw up | echar a perder | ruiner, gâter | durcheinanderbringen |
| to be rained out | cancelar por lluvia | ajourner, remettre | etwas abrufen wegen Regen |
| to go off the deep end | hacer algo precipitadamente | s'emporter, s'emballer | etwas ohne Achtung machen |
| to lose one's touch | perder la maña | perdre la main ou la touche | seine Geschicklichkeit zu verlieren |
| to have (something) going for (one) | tener algo bueno en marcha | être en grande demande | sehr erfolgreich sein |
| on the double! | ¡en el acto! | en vitesse!, sur le champ, au pas de course | schnell! |
| on hand | a mano | à portée de la main | verfübar |

| Lesson 33 | Spanish | French | German |
|---|---|---|---|
| to kick (something) around | debatir un asunto | ruminer, méditer | etwas überdenken, überlegen |
| on the ball | ser listo | alerte | am Ball sein |
| to say nothing of | ni hablar de | sans parler de | ohne zu sagen |
| to pull (oneself) together | calmarse, controlarse | se calmer, se ressaisir | sich zusammen-reissen |
| to be looking up | estar mejorando | être à la hausse, s'améliorer | besser werden |
| to kick a habit | dejar un vicio | se débarasser du vice | eine schlechte Angewohnheit aufgeben |
| to get into the swing of things | cogerle el golpe | se mettre en pleine activité | sich einführen |
| to cover up | encubrir | dissimuler | verdecken |
| to drop off | dispersarse | déposer | fallen drastisch |
| to get lost | perderse, levantar el vuelo | décamper | verschwinden |
| to go through channels | hacer algo debidamente | aller par entremise ou par voies | durch Mitteln gehen |
| to front for | hacerle frente por | faire figure ou façade | sich aufsetzen für |

| Lesson 34 | | | |
|---|---|---|---|
| to crack a book | abrir un libro, estudiar | ouvrir un livre, étudier | ein Buch lesen |
| to trade in | canjear, cambiar | échanger, faire le commerce de | umtauschen |
| face to face | cara a cara | face à face | von Angesicht zu Angesecht |
| to be with someone | estar de parte de, acordar | être avec quelqu'un | jemanden verstehen |
| to ease someone out | salir de (deshacerse) gradualmente de alguien | remplacer graduellement | einen Angestellten angenehm gehen lassen |
| to knock it off | dejar de | cesser immédiate-ment | aufhören |
| it figures | por supuesto, claro | c'est logique ou normal | es ist möglich |
| to fill (one) in | informar, orientar | mettre au courant | benachrichtigen |

|  | Spanish | French | German |
|---|---|---|---|
| to make one tick | motivar a | motiver, entraîner, pousser | was jemanden bewegt |
| to cover for | asumir los deberes de (otra persona) | couvrir, remplacer | für jemand anderes einstehen |
| to give (one) a break | darle oportunidad a alguien | donner une chance ou une opportunité | jemanden eine Chance geben |
| to bow out | salirse | demissionner | aufgeben |
| to cop out | evadir una responsabilidad | désister, éviter ses responsabilités | zurückziehen |

**Lesson 35**

|  | Spanish | French | German |
|---|---|---|---|
| to pin (something) on (one) | responsabilizar | accuser, jeter la faute sur quelqu'un | jemanden die Schuld für etwas geben |
| to get a rise out of (one) | obtener una reacción de alguien | mettre en colère | sich über jemanden amüsieren |
| to stick around | quedarse en el mismo sitio | ne pas quitter, demeurer | herumlungern |
| to pick up the tab | pagar la cuenta | financer, régler la facture | die Rechnung bezahlen |
| to call it a day | dejar de trabajar | terminer, la journée | Feierabend machen |
| to go to town | excederse | exagérer | etwas grundlich machen |
| to let (something) slide | dejar a un lado, evitar una responsabilidad | négliger, laisser aller les choses | etwas vernachlässigen |
| search me | ¡Que a mí no me pregunten! | ne pas avoir la moindre idée | ich weiss es nicht |
| can't help (but) | no puede menos que | ne pouvoir s'empêcher de | nicht anders Können |
| to live it up | darse vida de rico | mener la belle vie | hoch leben |
| to do a snow job | embaucar | tromper, décevoir, duper, abuser | jemanden betrügen |
| to have a voice in | tener voz en algún asunto | avoir une voix au chapitre | etwas zu zagen haben |

**Lesson 36**

|  | Spanish | French | German |
|---|---|---|---|
| to take another person at his word | confiar en la palabra de alguien | croire, prendre sur parole | sein Wort dafür nehmen |

|  | *Spanish* | *French* | *German* |
|---|---|---|---|
| to check in/out | llegar/irse | s'inscrire à/partir de | einchecken/ auschecken |
| to serve one's purpose | ser de utilidad, convenirle a uno | faire l'affaire | behilflich sein |
| in the worst way | sobremanera, en alto grado | à tout prix, désespérément | sehr, um alles |
| to want out | querer evadir una responsa- bilidad | vouloir la rupture ou la séparation | nichts mit zu tun haben |
| to buy it | creerlo | accepter, être séduit par l'idée | eine Idee annehmen |
| to line (someone or something) up | preparar algo o alguien | se trouver, aligner, réserver | besorgen |
| to lose (one's) cool | perder la paciencia | s'emporter, perdre son sang-froid | sich aufregen |
| to leave something open | dejar una salida abierta | garder ouvert ou en suspens | etwas verschieben |
| to turn (one) on | excitarlo a uno, entusiasmarlo | inspirer, répugner | grosse Interesse in etwas haben |
| to miss the boat | perder una oportunidad | rater l'opportunité, échouer | eine Gelegenheit verpassen |
| to dream up | inventar | avoir la brillante idée, rêver, imaginer | aufdenken |

## Lesson 37

|  |  |  |  |
|---|---|---|---|
| to throw (someone) a curve | confundir, cogerlo a uno desprevenido | confondre | jemanden in irreführen |
| to carry on | continuar | continuer | weitermachen |
| not on your life | ni hablar de eso | jamais de la vie | überhaupt nicht, nie |
| to cover a lot of ground | llevar mucho a cabo | couvrir beaucoup de terrain | sehr umfassend sein |
| to mind the store | cuidar de algo, ocuparse del negocio | surveiller la boutique | auf etwas Acht geben |
| to make waves | romper la calma, estorbar el orden | faire des histoires | etwas ausser Fassung bringen |
| to throw the book at | castigar severamente | être strict ou dur | sehr streng sein |

|  | *Spanish* | *French* | *German* |
|---|---|---|---|
| to clue (one) in | dar una pista, informar | tenir au courant | jemanden Auskunft |
| to be up for grabs | estar disponible, fácil de obtener | être disponible | zum Verkauf geben sein |
| to catch up | ponerse al tanto | rattraper | nachholen |
| big deal | gran cosa | grande chose, (se croire) quelqu'un important | grosse Sache, sehr wichtig |

### Lesson 38

|  |  |  |  |
|---|---|---|---|
| to land on (one's) feet | caer de pie como un gato | tomber à quatres pattes | sich unversehrt erholen |
| to dish out | dar algo en abundancia, derrochar, dar a manos llenas | être désagréable | jemanden kritisieren |
| to get to another person | hacer entender a alguien | s'entendre avec | jemanden verstehen |
| each other/one another | uno al otro | l'un l'autre | gegenseitig |
| to bug one | fastidiar, molestar, fregar | ennuyer, embêter, importuner | jemanden plagen |
| to ask for | provocar, incitar | chercher des histoires | aufreisen |
| to live in | dormir donde uno trabaja | coucher à la maison | einwohnen |
| to have what it takes | tener las aptitudes necesarias para | avoir les aptitudes nécessaires | richtig für etwas sein |
| of course | desde luego | bien sûr | selbstverständ-lich |
| to get out from under | salir a flote | surmonter ses pertes | sich finanziell erholen |
| to take the bull by the horns | enfrentarse con | être déterminé, décisif | etwas mit Bestimmung machen |
| to give one a big hand | aplaudir efusivamente | applaudir fortement | Beifall spenden |

### Lesson 39

|  |  |  |  |
|---|---|---|---|
| to goof off | vaguear | être oisif | faulenzen |
| what with | debido a | à cause de | wegen |
| to talk back | protestar | rétorquer | dagegenreden |
| to be in | estar a la moda | être à la page | modern sein |
| to date | hasta ahora | á ce jour | bis jetzt |

|  | *Spanish* | *French* | *German* |
|---|---|---|---|
| to top something | ganarle, sobrepasar una meta | dépasser | etwas übertreffen |
| dry run | ensayo | faire des essais ou des épreuves | eine Probe |
| to play something by ear | tocar algo de oído | jouer par oreille | ein Stück Musik auswending spielen, etwas verschieben um zu sehen was sich entwickelt |
| to get (step) out of line | faltar al reglamento | avoir une mauvaise conduite | ungehorsam sein |
| fringe benefit | beneficio marginal | bénéfice marginal | etwas wertvolles das ein Angestellter bekommt ausser dem Gehalt |
| to fix (someone or something) up | arreglar algo o alguien, concordar una cita | choisir, réparer | etwas aufsetzen für jemanden, etwas reparieren |
| to be had | ser engañado, timado, estafado | être roulé, trompé, dupé, volé | beschwindelt sein |

# INDEX